OUT OF JOINT

C000143387

A Sheffield Theatres and Out of Joint Co-Production

CLOSE QUARTERS

by **Kate Bowen**

Thursday 25 October 2018 – Saturday 10 November 2018
Studio Theatre, Sheffield

CLOSE QUARTERS

by **Kate Bowen**

CAST

Sergeant John Adeyemi, Infantry	**Bradley Banton**
Private Sarah Findlay, Infantry	**Ruby Barker**
Private Clare Davies, Infantry	**Sophie Melville**
Captain Anna Sands, Intelligence Corps	**Kathryn O'Reilly**
Private Alison Cormack, Infantry	**Chloe-Ann Tylor**
Lance Corporal Brian Armstrong, Infantry	**Dylan Wood**

PRODUCTION TEAM

Director	**Kate Wasserberg**
Designer	**Max Jones**
Lighting Designer	**Sarah Jane Shiels**
Composer and Sound Designer	**Dyfan Jones**
Casting Directors	**Jenkins McShane Casting** CDG
Fight and Movement Directors	**Rachel Bown-Williams and Ruth Cooper-Brown of RC-Annie Ltd.**
Dramaturg	**Catriona Craig**
Associate Designer	**Ruth Hall**
Assistant Director	**Jesse Haughton-Shaw**
Production Manager	**Stephanie Balmforth**
Stage Manager	**Katie Bosomworth**
Deputy Stage Manager	**Bethan Dawson**
Assistant Stage Manager	**Hannah Birtwistle-Crossland**

CAST BIOGRAPHIES

BRADLEY BANTON – SERGEANT JOHN ADEYEMI
Bradley graduated from Bristol Old Vic Theatre School in 2017.

Theatre credits include: *The Two Gentlemen of Verona, Our Country's Good, The Island, Someone Who'll Watch Over Me, A Midsummer Night's Dream, The Laramie Project, Days of Significance, The School for Scandal, Twelfth Night, The Vortex* (Bristol Old Vic Theatre School).

Television and film credits include: *Vera* (ITV); *His House* (New Regency) and *Judy* (Pathé).

This is Bradley's professional stage debut.

RUBY BARKER – PRIVATE SARAH FINDLAY
Theatre credits include: *York Mystery Plays* and *Mankind* (Hidden Theatre Company).

Television and film credits include: *Wolfblood, Biscuits* (CBBC); *Doctors* (BBC) and *How to Stop a Recurring Dream* (Rattling Snake Productions).

This is Ruby's professional stage debut.

SOPHIE MELVILLE – PRIVATE CLARE DAVIES
Recent theatre credits include: *Pops* (Young Vic); *No One Will Tell Me How to Start a Revolution* (Hampstead); *The Divide, Pagans* (Old Vic); *Low Level Panic* (Orange Tree); *2066* (Almeida); *Blackbird* (The Other Room); *Insignificance, Under Milk Wood* (Theatr Clwyd); *Iphigenia in Splott* (National Theatre, New York transfer, Berlin transfer, Sherman/Edinburgh Fringe); *Romeo and Juliet* (Sherman); *The Shape of Things, 'Tis Pity She's a Whore, See How They Run* (Theatre by the Lake) and *Romeo and Juliet* (Sam Wanamaker Festival).

Television and film credits include: *The Missing 2* (BBC); *Canaries; Cupidity* (Film London) and *Telling Tales* (BBC).

KATHRYN O'REILLY – CAPTAIN ANNA SANDS
Kathryn trained at LAMDA.

Previous work for Out of Joint includes: *A View from Islington North* (Arts); *Our Country's Good* (Bolton Octagon/international tour/Guthrie, USA/Royal Alexander, Toronto); *Andersen's English* (Hampstead) and *Mixed Up North* (Bolton Octagon).

Theatre credits include: *YOU* (VAULT Festival); *Arms and the Man* (Watford Palace Theatre); *Caught (*Arcola); *In the Fog, Allotments* (Optik); *Bluebird* (Space); *Blank* (Lakeside Theatre); *hamlet is dead. no gravity* (Arcola); *Rift* (Brewhouse); *The Golden Dragon* (Drum Theatre Royal Plymouth); *A Christmas Carol* (Trafalgar Studios 2); *Love on the Tracks* (Soho Studio); *Oedipus* (national tour); *Rumplestiltskin* (Wimbledon) and *Don Juan* (Rose).

Television and film credits include: *Call the Midwife, Holby City, Doctors* (BBC); *The Last Trace* (UFA Fiction Ltd); *Grantchester, Lewis* (ITV); *The Bill* (Talkback Thames); *Rough Justice* (Hewland International); *The Little Stranger* (Potboiler Productions); *Klink Klank, Zebra Crossing* (Crown Films); *Halal Harry* (21st February Films); *Crystallisation* (Sophia Films); *Rare Beasts* (Western Edge Pictures) and *random* (Film4/HillBilly Films).

CHLOE-ANN TYLOR – PRIVATE ALISON CORMACK
Theatre credits include: *Hansel and Gretel*, *Trainspotting* (Citizens Theatre); *The Strange Case of Jekyll & Hyde* (Royal Conservatoire of Scotland); *The Merchant of Venice* (Bard in the Botanics) and *Titus Andronicus* (Dundee Rep).

DYLAN WOOD – LANCE CORPORAL BRIAN ARMSTRONG
Dylan is a recent graduate of Bristol Old Vic Theatre School.

Theatre credits include: *Teddy* (Watermill/UK tour); *Electric Eden* (Shanghai Arts Festival/Not Too Tame Theatre Company); *King Lear*, *Snow Queen* (Bristol Old Vic); *The Tempest*, *The Wind in the Willows*, *Julius Caesar*, *The Beaux Stratagem*, *We've got to get to Bethlehem*, *Three Sisters*, *Henry IV*, *The School for Scandal*, *The Events*, *Flare Path*, *The Promise* (Bristol Old Vic Theatre School) and *The Drowsy Chaperone*, *Bye Bye Birdie* (Dance School of Scotland).

Film and radio credits include: *In the Night*, *Falco* (Bristol Old Vic Theatre School).

PRODUCTION BIOGRAPHIES

KATE BOWEN – PLAYWRIGHT
Kate was the 2012 winner of the annual New Writers Award (Playwright's Studio Scotland) and a participant in the 2013 Traverse 50 programme at the Traverse Theatre, Edinburgh. She was awarded a place on the Channel 4 Playwrights' Scheme in 2016, a Starter for Ten residency from the National Theatre of Scotland in 2017 and was invited to be part of the BBC Writersroom Scotland's first Drama Writers Group in 2018.

Writing credits include: *The Prize Fighter* (Traverse Theatre/short audio play); *The Lawyers* (Three Minute Theatre for Play, Pie and a Pint, Glasgow) and *Super Sunday* (Five Minute Theatre for National Theatre of Scotland).

This is her first full length play to be produced.

KATE WASSERBERG – DIRECTOR
Kate is the Artistic Director of Out of Joint and has previously been the Artistic Director of the Other Room and Associate Director at Theatr Clwyd and Finborough Theatre.

Theatre credits include: *Rita, Sue and Bob Too* (Out of Joint/Bolton Octagon/Royal Court/tour); *Seanmhair, Play/Silence, Sand, Blasted* and *The Dying of Today* (Other Room); *The Rise and Fall of Little Voice, Insignificance, All My Sons, Aristocrats, Salt, Root and Roe, Glengarry Glen Ross, Last Christmas, Bruised, Roots, Gaslight, Dancing at Lughnasa* (Theatr Clwyd); *Pieces* (Theatr Clwyd/Brits Off Broadway Festival); *The Glass Menagerie* (Theatre Clwyd/tour); *A History of Falling Things* (Theatre Clwyd/Sherman); *The Man* (Finborough/tour); *Songs of York, Little Madam, The Representative, I Wish to Die Singing, The New Morality, Mirror Teeth* (Finborough); *Barnbow Canaries* (West Yorkshire Playhouse); *Ten Weeks* (Royal Welsh College of Music and Drama/Paines Plough); *Saturday Night Forever* (Aberystwyth Arts Centre/Edinburgh); *Contractions* (Waking Exploits); *The Knowledge* (Royal Court); *2007 Schools Festival* (Young Vic) and *Switzerland* (Hightide Festival).

Kate is the co-editor (with playwright Tim Price) of *Contemporary Welsh Plays* published by Bloomsbury. She has been a senior reader for the National Theatre Playwriting Prize and the Bruntwood Prize for Playwriting.

MAX JONES – DESIGNER
For Sheffield Theatres, credits include: *Love and Information* and *Queen Coal*.

Credits include: *Shakespeare in Love* (Theatre Royal Bath); *Meek* (Headlong); *A Streetcar Named Desire, Orpheus Descending* (Bunkamura, Tokyo); *The House They Grew Up In* (Headlong/Chichester Festival Theatre); *The Hypocrite* (Royal Shakespeare Company/Hull Truck); *The Shoemakers Holiday, Merry Wives of Windsor* (Royal Shakespeare Company); *True West* (Citizens, Glasgow/Tricycle); *Trainspotting, A Day in the Death of Joe Egg, The Caretaker* (Citizens, Glasgow); *Pride and Prejudice* (Regent's Park Open Air Theatre/UK tour); *The York Mystery Plays* (York Minster); *The Crucible, Brilliant Adventures, Miss Julie* (Royal Exchange Theatre, Manchester); *A Time to Reap, Spur of the Moment* (Royal Court); *Così fan tutte* (Welsh National Opera/UK tour); *Little Shop of Horrors, Educating Rita, Glengarry Glen Ross, Bruised, A Doll's House, Dancing at Lughnasa, Blackthorn, A Small Family Business, Mary Stuart, Measure for Measure, Two Princes, The Grapes Of Wrath* (Theatre Clwyd); *The Broken Heart, The Tempest* (Shakespeare's Globe); *Play Strindberg* (Ustinov, Bath); *Much Ado About Nothing* (NPAC, Japan); *Of Mice and Men* (West Yorkshire Playhouse); *The Winter's Tale* (Regent's Park Open Air Theatre); *Twist of Gold* (Polka); *Fatherland* (Gate/Munich); *The Hard Man* (King's Edinburgh/ UK tour); *Party* (Arts); *Mad Forest* (Battersea Arts Centre); *Dumb Show* (New Vic, Stoke); *Sweeney Todd* (Welsh National Youth Opera); *The Lady from the Sea* (Theatre Genedlaethol Cymru); *Blasted* (The Other Room); *The Life of Ryan... And Ronnie* (Script Cymru) *and Salt Meets Wound* (Theatre503).

Max is a graduate of the Royal Welsh College of Music and Drama in Cardiff and he was formerly an Associate Artist at Theatre Clwyd under Terry Hands.

SARAH JANE SHIELS – LIGHTING DESIGNER

SJ began designing lighting in Dublin Youth Theatre, completing a BA in Drama and Theatre Studies 2006 (Trinity), and the Rough Magic Seeds3 programme 2006 – 2008.

Lighting design credits include: *Portrait of the Artist as a Young Man*, *The Effect*, *Everything Between Us*, *The Critic*, *The House Keeper*, *Plaza Suite* (Rough Magic); *FRNKNSTN* (Theatre Lovett); *Dolores*, *Soldier Still*, *Dusk Ahead* (Junk Ensemble); *Where We Live* (THISISPOPBABY); *East Belfast Boy/Everyday I Wake Up Hopeful* (Prime Cut); *Radio Rosario* (Little John Nee); *Jimmy's Hall*, *The Remains of Maise Duggan*, *Town is Dead* (Abbey); *Dublin Oldschool* (Project Arts Centre); *PALS*, *The Boys of Foley Street*, *Laundry*, *World's End Lane*, *Basin* (ANU Productions) and *This Beach*, *Have I No Mouth*, *The Blue Boy*, *Silver Stars* (Brokentalkers).

Set and lighting design credits include: *BEES!*, *Jockey*, *CARE*, *Farm*, *Follow* (WillFredd Theatre); *How to Keep an Alien* (Sonya Kelly/Rough Magic) and *It Folds* (Junk Ensemble/Brokentalkers).

DYFAN JONES – COMPOSER AND SOUND DESIGNER

Dyfan trained at Kingston University and The Guildhall School of Music and Drama. He has over 25 years of experience working as a Composer, Musical Director and Sound Designer.

Theatre credits include: *Shakespeare in Love* (Theatre Royal Bath/tour); *Amedee*, *Treasure Island* (Birmingham Rep); *A View from Islington North*, *All That Fall* (Out of Joint); *Barnbow Canaries* (West Yorkshire Playhouse); *Love & Money* (Waking Exploits); *Before I Leave* (National Theatre Wales); *Crouch, Touch, Pause, Engage* (National Theatre of Wales/Out of Joint); *The Rise and Fall of Little Voice*, *Insignificance*, *Cyrano de Bergerac*, *My People*, *Little Shop of Horrors*, *All My Sons*, *Mimosa*, *Not About Heroes*, *Portrait of the Artist as a Young Dog*, *Season's Greetings*, *Sky Hawk*, *Rape of the Fair Country*, *Humbug!*, *A Feast of Festive Fun*, *Flora's War*, *Thinking Out Loud*, *Tall Tales*, *Festen*, *Great Expectations*, *Yesterday*, *Twilight Tales*, *Drowned Out*, *Measure for Measure*, *A Midsummer Night's Dream*, *A Toy Epic*, *Grapes of Wrath*, *Tales from Europe*, *Tales from Small Nations*, *To Kill a Mockingbird*, *Song of the Earth*, *Abigail's Party*, *Hosts of Rebecca*, *The Way It Was*, *Home Front*, *Oh! What a Lovely War* (Theatr Clwyd); *Contractions* (Iain Goosey/Chapter); *Still Life* (Mappa Mundi); *Seanmhair*, *Play*, *Silence*, *Blasted*, *A Good Clean Heart* (The Other Room); *The Magic Porridge Pot*, *The Ugly Duckling*, *The Snow Tiger*, *Corina Pavlova*, *A Family Affair*, *Say it with Flowers* (Sherman); *Beyond Borders*, *Mimosa*, *No Other Day Like Today*, *Canrif/Century*, *The Magnificent Myths of the Mabinogi* (National Youth Theatre of Wales); *Jack and the Beanstalk* (Stafford Gatehouse Theatre); *Milwr yn y Meddwl*, *Macbeth*, *Nansi*, *Pan Oedd y Byd yn Fach*, *Blodeuwedd*, *Pridd*, *Chwalfa*, *Pan Oedd y Byd yn Fach*, *Dyled Eileen*, *Spring Awakening*, *House of America*, *2110/Yn Y Trên*, *The Caretaker*, *Esther* (Theatr Genedlaethol Cymru); *Cider With Rosie*, *Cyrano*, *Skylight* (Theatre West Glamorgan) and *Amdani*, *Indian Country* (Sgript Cymru).

Film and television credits include: *Boj & Buddies* (Bait); *Llanargollen* (Twt/S4C); *Soli and Mo* (CITV/S4C/Al Jazeera); *Cwm Teg* (Dinamo Productions for S4C), *Abadas* (Cbeebies); *Dragon's Eye*, *Children in Need*, *Close to You*, *Wales Yesterday*, *A Christmas in Clay*, *Belonging*, *Just Up Your Street*, *The Indian Doctor*, *Voices*, *Save Our World* (BBC); *Teulu* (Boomerang); *Iechyd Da!*, *31/12/99* (Bracan), *Cloud Babies* (S4C); *Pobol y Cwm* (BBC) and *Jara, Pam Fi Duw?*, *Bydd yn Wrol* (HTV/Carlton).

JENKINS MCSHANE CASTING/LUCY JENKINS CDG & SOOKI MCSHANE CDG – CASTING DIRECTORS

For Out of Joint: *Our Country's Good*.

Other recent theatre credits include: *The Last Ship* (Northern Stage/tour); *The Kite Runner* (West End/tour); *The Comedy About a Bank Robbery* (West End/tour); *The Play that Goes Wrong* (West End/tour); *The Red Lion, Bomber's Moon* (Trafalgar); *War Horse* (West End/tour); *Jekyll & Hyde* (Rose/tour); *Cathy* (Cardboard Citizens); *Home Truths, La Ronde* (Bunker); *Clear White Light, My Romantic History* (Live Theatre); *A Short History of Tractors in Ukrainian* and *Mighty Atoms* (Hull Truck); *Alice in Winterland* (Rose); *The Quiet House* (Park); *The Divided Laing* (Arcola); *Wet House* (Soho) and *Serpent's Tooth* (Almeida).

Film credits include: *For Love or Money*; *Widow's Walk*; *The Comedian's Guide to Survival* and *Bliss!*

RC-ANNIE LTD. RACHEL BOWN-WILLIAMS AND RUTH COOPER-BROWN – FIGHT AND MOVEMENT DIRECTORS

Established in 2005 by Rachel Bown-Williams and Ruth Cooper-Brown, RC-ANNIE is the UK's leading Dramatic Violence Company.

Theatre credits include: *Emilia, Othello, The Secret Theatre, Boudica, Lions and Tigers, Much Ado About Nothing, Twelfth Night, The White Devil, Comus, Imogen* (Shakespeare's Globe); *The Little Matchgirl* (Bristol Old Vic/Shakespeare's Globe); *A Very, Very, Very Dark Matter* (The Bridge); *Wise Children* (Wise Children/Old Vic); *Company* (Elliot Harper Productions at The Gielgud Theatre); *Europe* (Leeds Playhouse); *Tartuffe, The Duchess of Malfi, Salome, Snow in Midsummer* (Royal Shakespeare Company); *God of Carnage, The Price, Switzerland* and *Dusty* (Theatre Royal Bath); *A Monster Calls, Woyzeck* (Old Vic); *Hogarth's Progress, My Brilliant Friend* (Rose, Kingston); *The Village* (Theatre Royal Stratford East); *Girl on a Train, Sunshine on Leith, The Lion, The Witch and The Wardrobe, Barnbow Canaries, Great Expectations, Richard III* (West Yorkshire Playhouse); *A Clockwork Orange* (Liverpool Everyman); *Common, Ugly Lies the Bone, Peter Pan, The Threepenny Opera, The James Plays* (co-production with National Theatre of Scotland and Edinburgh International Festival) and *Cleansed* (National Theatre).

CATRIONA CRAIG – DRAMATURG

Catriona Craig is the Literary Manager for Out of Joint. Former Literary Manager of The Finborough Theatre she has worked as a script editor, reader and artistic associate for organisations such as BBC Comedy, BBC Writersroom, Parallel Films, the National Theatre, Love&Madness, The Verity Bargate Award, The Orange Tree Theatre, RTÉ and TG4 in Ireland. She is also Senior Lecturer in Performing Arts at Buckinghamshire New University.

RUTH HALL – ASSOCIATE DESIGNER

Ruth Hall is a freelance set and costume designer for theatre in the UK and abroad, London based, originally from Bristol. She trained at the Royal Welsh College of Music and Drama, achieving a First Class BA Hons in Theatre Design; she was selected as a Trainee Designer to join the Royal Shakespeare Company's apprenticeship 2005–6.

Design credits include: *Big Aftermath after Small Disclosure* (Actors Touring Company); *Sonny* (ArtsEd); *46 Beacon* (Trafalgar Studios); *Macbeth* (Carephilly Castle/Theatr Genedlaethol); *Blackbird* (The Other Room); *Little Shop of Horrors* (co-design/Theatre Clwyd); *Y Fenyw Ddaeth o'r Môr* (co-design/Theatr Genedlaethol Cymru); *Blasted* (co-design/The Other Room); *Play Strindberg* (co-design/Ustinov); *Contractions* (co-design/Chapter Arts Centre); *Fijiland* (Southwark Playhouse); *Sky Hawk, Salt, Root and Roe* (Theatr Clwyd); *Altogether Now* (North Wall Theatre); *Pridd* (Theatr Genedlaethol); *Noah* (Theatre On The Fly, Chichester); *The Road To Mecca* (Arcola) and *Tale of Two Cities* (Royal & Derngate/tour).

Costume design credits include: *Educating Rita* and *Glengarry Glen Ross* (Theatr Clwyd).

Associate Designer credits include: *Shakespeare in Love* (Bath Theatre Royal/tour); *A Streetcar Named Desire* (Theatre Cocoon, Tokyo); *York Mystery Plays* (site specific in York Minster Cathedral); *Orpheus Descending* (Theatre Cocoon, Tokyo); *Of Mice and Men* (West Yorkshire Playhouse); *Crime and Punishment* (Citizens, Glasgow); *Henry VI Trilogy, Romeo and Juliet, The Tempest, The Winter's Tale, Pericles* (Royal Shakespeare Company); *Zorro* (Garrick) and *London Road* (National Theatre).

Film Art Department Assistant credits include: *London Road* (Cuba Pictures).

JESSE HAUGHTON-SHAW – ASSISTANT DIRECTOR

Jesse Haughton-Shaw is Resident Assistant Director at Sheffield Theatres, and is currently studying for an MFA in Theatre Directing at Birkbeck College.

As director, credits include: *Small Traumas* (writer/The Lion and Unicorn); *Cain* (co-writer/Hope); *The Jewish Wife* (Stonecrabs Young Directors' Festival/The Albany); *Can't Stand Up for Falling Down* (co-director); *The Maids* (theSpace, Edinburgh).

Whilst training, credits include: *Hedda Gabler* (ADC Theatre Cambridge); *The House of Bernarda Alba* (Corpus Playroom, Cambridge).

PRODUCTION CREDITS

Costume Supervisor
Merle Richards-Wright
Lighting Programmer
Phil Baines
Airborne Sound Effects Design & Creation
Nick Greenhill

Scenic Artists
Rory Davis
Stephanie Etahadi
Dave Gillan
Ruth Hall

Performance Staff

Lighting Operator
Phil Baines

Contractors and Suppliers
Harrogate Theatre Scenic Services
Sheffield Theatres Workshop
Blooming Artificial
Stage Sound Services
Quantum SFX

Sheffield Theatres would like to thank: Curve Theatre Leicester, Nigel Filmer at Jay Jays Genuine Army Surplus Sheffield, Peli Protector Cases supplied by Peli Products UK, Sheffield Tree Care Ltd., Smart Student Accommodation, Thomas Dornan Ltd, Tim Ball of Volkswagen Oldham, Sheffield Tank and Drum Company and Sheffield City Council

Out of Joint would like to extend our thanks to the following for their support: Lois Chimimba, Jack Tarlton, Jodie Whittaker, Naveed Khan, Noof McEwan, Sian Howard, Sophie Melville, Tok Stephen, Javaad Alipoor, Suba Das, Gabriella Bird, Steve Nash and Steffi Holtz.

Kate Bowen would like to give special thanks to the following:
Jamie Howard, S Wright, Mark Abraham, Vanessa Freestone, Sarah Tierney, Bianca Lawson, Lu Kemp, Frances Poet, Jim Hutchison, Rosemary McHale, Trevor Bowen and Olivia Frigerio.

sheffield theatres
crucible lyceum studio

Sheffield Theatres is the largest producing theatre complex outside of London, home to three theatres: the Crucible, the Studio and the Lyceum. In recognition of its success in creating new work, its bold approach to new classics and accessible ticketing policy, the Theatre was named Regional Theatre of the Year 2017, by *The Stage*, for an unprecedented third time, adding to wins in 2013 and 2014.

The company produces a diverse programme of work, spanning a range of genres: classical revivals, new work, large-scale musicals and innovative and immersive theatre experiences. It presents the best shows currently on tour in the UK and works with theatre artists locally and nationally to nurture and develop new creative talent.

Sheffield Theatres' 2018/19 season includes: the riotous romantic musical comedy *Kiss Me, Kate*, the world premiere of *Standing at the Sky's Edge* with music by Richard Hawley, Githa Sowerby's classic *Rutherford and Son*, *hang* by debbie tucker green and a major new production of *Life of Pi*.

Combining classic and contemporary programming with a bold and ambitious approach, Sheffield Theatres has firmly established itself as one of the country's leading theatres.

 @CrucibleTheatre
@SheffieldLyceum

 @Sheffield_Theatres

 Sheffield Theatres

sheffieldtheatres.co.uk

Staff

Chief Executive **Dan Bates**
Artistic Director **Robert Hastie**

Senior Management Team
Communications & Fundraising Director **Claire Murray**
Finance & Resources Director **Bookey Oshin**
Producer **Caroline Dyott**

Administration Team
HR Manager **Michael Bailey***
HR Officer **Lorna Knight**
Assistant to Chief Executive & Artistic Director **Jackie Pass**

Box Office Team
Sales & Customer Care Manager **Caroline Laurent**
Deputy Sales Managers **Kate Fisher, Louise Renwick**
Sales and Customer Care Supervisor **Claire Fletcher***
Access and Sales Supervisor **Paul Whitley**
Sales and Group Supervisor **Ian Caudwell***
Sales Assistants **Carrie Askew, Sue Cooper***, Alistair Eades,
Sally Field, Faye Hardaker, Pat Holland***, Charlotte
Keyworth, Rebecca McQuillan, Christine Monaghan***,
Joe Philpott, Heather Reynolds, Christine Smith,
Irene Stewart, Katy Wainwright, Hannah Winnell

Communications Team
Communications Manager **Rachel Nutland**
Deputy Communications Manager **Oliver Eastwood**
Media Officer **Ellie Greenfield**
Communications Officers **Laura Bloor, Alice Dale, Anna Lord**
Communications Officer (Maternity Cover) **Alice Dale**
Communications Trainee **Keir Shields**
Programmer **Mikey Cook**
National Press Support **Kate Morley PR**

Customer Services Team
General Bars & Catering Manager **Andrew Cooper***
House Manager **Debbie Smith***
Crucible Corner Manager **Kris Addy**
Head Chef **Natalie Bailey**
Sous Chef **Daniel Lockwood**
Chef De Partie **Daniel Lockwood**
Commis Chef **Antonio Massuno**
Kitchen Assistant **Dean Fox**
Apprentice Chef **Tom Jacobs**
Events Coordinator **Lianne Froggatt**
Events Management Trainee **Jasmine Chong**
Catering & Bars Shift Leaders **Aeddan Lockett, Archie Ward***
Café Supervisor **Joanne Murrison**
Duty Managers **Sue Cooper***, Andrea Eades, Lucy Hockney,
Adrian Tolson, Tracy Waldron**
Firepersons **Denise Hobart, Suzanne Palzer, Lucy Procter,
Heather Reynolds, Jon Robinson**
Cellar Person **Robin Atkinson**
Restaurant Assistants **Chris Andrade, Rebecca Davidson,
William Stroie, Holly Williams**
Catering Assistants **Megan Archer, Carrie Askew, Rosy
Asquith, Pippa Atkinson, Toni Brown, Caryl Carson,
Jessica Chittenden, Leslie Cooper, James Doolan, Jenny
Everson, Judi Flint, Alex Glentworth, Jess Goh, Joanne
Hall, Christina Higgins, Nicole Hodder, Sandra Holmes,
Juliet Ibberson, Sue Jones***, Holly Kempton, Gregory
Knowles, Hannah Lamare, Lauren Lomas, Sarah Marshall,
Nuala Meely, Sarah Moat, Tom Nugent, Fabian O'Farrell,
Lois Pearson, Ioana Radulescu, Cyndi Richardson,
Abby Russell, Louise Sanderson, Liz Sayles, Richard
Sidebottom, Harris Slater, Grace Parker-Slater, Grace
Smith, William Stroie, Andrea Suter, Claire Sweeney,
Jonathon Syer, Jack Weston, Annette Williamson,
Isa Wood**

Front of House Assistants **Anne Archer, Hester Astell, Steve
Athey***, Courtney Ball, Belinda Beasley, Jean Bennett,
Marianne Bolton, George Bowley, Mari Bullock, Ann
Butler***, Julie Cartwright, Jane Challenger, Megan Clarke,
Lilli Connelly, Vicky Cooper, Gillian Crossland, John
Daggett, Marie Darling, Sandra Eddison, Maureen Foster,
Emma Gibson, Sara Godbehere, Jake Goode, Nick Henry,
Denise Hobart, Lucy Hockney, Abigail Ivall, Scott Johnson,
Hannah Jones, Charlotte Keyworth, Beth Kinross, Alex
Lamb, Martha Lamb, Diane Lilleyman, Margaret Lindley,
Emma Lomas, Aimee Marshall, James Middleton, Sylvia
Mortimer***, Susie Newman, Cat Oldham, Kourtney Owen,
Liz Owen, Susanne Palzer, Jodie Passey, Ann Phenix, Nate
Powell, Ruth Price, Lucy Procter, Richard Rawson***,
Heather Reynolds, Jonathan Robinson, Dionne Sulph,
Adrian Tolson, Bev Turner, Tracy Waldron, Christine
Wallace, Eleanor White, Joe White, Stuart Williamson***

Facilities Team
Buildings Manager **John Bates**
Buildings Officer **Rob Chapman**
Maintenance Supervisor **Julian Simpson***
Maintenance Technician **Richard Powell-Pepper**
House Assistants **David Hayes, Katie Howard, Amy Jenner,
James McCready, Grace Staples-Burton, Jacob Ross,
Kate Wilkinson, Richard Winks***
Receptionist/Telephonist **Angela Ridgeway***
Head Cleaners **Jenny Hardy***, Karen Walker***
Cleaners **Kelly Baxter, Susan Baxter, Tracey Bourabaa,
Louisa Cottingham, Yvonne Dwyer***, Gail Fox, Jill Francis,
Lynn Highton, Diane Sayles, Diane Turton, Andrew Wild**

Finance Team
Finance Managers **Samantha Pentland, Christine Drabble**
Finance Officer **Lesley Barkworth-Short***
Payroll & Finance Officer **Jean Deakin***,
Finance Assistants **Lindsey Copley-Dunn, Faye Ellames**
Finance Trainee **Dami Fajinmi**

Fundraising Team
Fundraising Manager **Abigail Walton**
Individual Giving Officer **Leah Woffenden**
Partnerships Officer **Laura Winson**
Individual Giving Officer (Interim) **Siobhan Halpin**
Membership Officer (Interim) **James Ashfield** (*This post is
made possible by the Weston Jerwood Creative Bursaries
programme*)

Learning Team
Creative Projects Manager **Emily Hutchinson**
Learning Project Worker – Education **Georgina Stone**
Fun Palaces Ambassador **Beverley Nunn**
Learning Workshop Assistants **Joe Barber, Tommi Bryson,
Lois Pearson**

◘UT OF JOINT

Dauntless. Political. Joyous.

'A blast of real life'
Ann Treneman, *The Times*

Out of Joint develops, produces and tours political, humane and socially engaged shows of outstanding quality, that spark and enrich conversations around the UK and the world.

We believe that artists should be at the frontier of new ideas, and champion underrepresented voices and perspectives. The company invests substantially in the development of writers, directors, actors and audiences to ensure that new plays are thriving, presenting them alongside timely revivals that reinvigorate familiar texts.

Through partnerships and touring, the company engages as wide an audience as possible across the UK. With the strong belief that theatre should be the start of political conversation, Out of Joint commissions productions that open hearts and minds through fearless writing. Our co-producers include the Royal Court, the National Theatre and Sheffield Theatres.

> 'Brief, hilarious, angry, and blazing with honesty, Andrea Dunbar's *Rita, Sue and Bob Too* bursts onto the stage of the Citizens' like a play from the past that is somehow more contemporary than most plays written today… Kate Wasserberg's production captures all the pace, wit and brutality of the story.'
>
> **Joyce MacMillan, *The Scotsman***

Out of Joint is proud to be touring Andrea Dunbar's ground-breaking play *Rita, Sue and Bob Too*. Raw, honest and affecting, the play has lost none of its shocking realism that made it a modern classic. The provocative, timeless play will return to stages across the UK in spring 2019.

In association with Oxford Playhouse and Northampton theatre, Out of Joint presents a poignant adaptation of Kazuo Ishiguro's literary classic, *The Remains of the Day*. The tale of love, loyalty, and duty is reimagined by one of Britain's most exciting writers, Barney Norris. The play will open at Royal & Derngate Theatre, Northampton and will tour from March 2019.

Support Our Work

Out of Joint is a registered charity that serves the national theatre community through touring. Whilst we are partly funded by Arts Council England, we rely on donations to continue our work in taking quality productions across the UK. If you would like to talk about becoming one of our supporters, please get in touch with hello@outofjoint.co.uk

The Andrea Project

Out of Joint offers a diverse programme of workshops to nurture the playwriting skills of teenagers and young adults. In memory of playwright Andrea Dunbar, we invest in the writers of tomorrow, who may not have hailed from backgrounds historically associated with theatre. We actively seek voices from all communities and give them a platform to explore their experiences.

We would like to extend our special thanks to our donors who have made The Andrea Project possible: Rishi Dastidar, Michael Langan, Tatty Hennessy, Gayle Appleyard of Gagarin Studio, Gemma Bell, Yvonne Gallagher, Nick Gill, Jackie Daly, Lucy Foster, Kris Stewart, Dan Slipper, Alex Jones, Victoria Sadler, Kathryn Gardner, Aradhna Tayal, Adelle Stripe, Jennifer Derbyshire, Chi Chan and Kerstin Mogull.

Out of Joint

3 Thane Works, Thane Villas, London, N7 7NU
Tel: +44 (0)207 609 0207
Email: hello@outofjoint.co.uk
Web: www.outofjoint.co.uk

Supported using public funding by
**ARTS COUNCIL
ENGLAND**

AUTHOR'S NOTE

Close Quarters is the first full length play of mine to be produced and has been a collaborative effort. I owe a lot to the weighty talents of Kate Wasserberg and Catriona Craig, who challenged, inspired and worked with me tirelessly to create a script that I wouldn't have made in this way without their combined energies and wisdom. I want to thank them for the patience, support and knowledge they've given me and the play.

During the time of writing, the British army had only just opened up ground close combat infantry roles to women, and this is a work of fiction imagining a time in the future, the first tour of duty for three female recruits.

The job of the infantry is to close with and kill the enemy, often at close quarters. The British government making the decision that women could apply to do the job was a controversial one. But the way the public debate about the decision was conducted revealed more about the ongoing misunderstandings in our culture of what it is to be female than it did about the merits of the decision itself. Right or wrong, or somewhere in between – the conversation about the decision informs the play but doesn't drive it.

What in fact fuels the play is my deep interest in the individual women. Why would they choose to do the job? How will they cope with being a tiny minority? What strategies will they use to adapt to a world which isn't built for them and is wary of what they represent? All the characters in the play have to deal with these things and find ways to fit in, fit around each other, meet their own needs and succeed without losing or damaging what they love.

Kate Bowen

CLOSE QUARTERS

Kate Bowen

Characters

PRIVATE SARAH FINDLAY, *infantry, early twenties*
PRIVATE ALISON CORMACK, *infantry, early twenties*
LANCE CORPORAL BRIAN ARMSTRONG, *infantry,*
    early twenties
PRIVATE CLARE DAVIES, *infantry, early twenties*
SERGEANT JOHN ADEYEMI, *infantry, late twenties*
CAPTAIN ANNA SANDS, *Intelligence Corps, late thirties*

Note on Text

A dash (–) indicates a hesitation.

A forward slash (/) indicates one character is being interrupted by another.

This text went to press before the end of rehearsals and so may differ slightly from the play as performed.

Prologue

2032.

FINDLAY *is standing in a pool of light on a dark stage. She is wearing combat uniform though it's too dark to tell which rank.*

She looks towards a doorway, stage left, from which a sliver of light is shining.

FINDLAY. I'd never even heard of Estonia before we got sent there.
I expect they'd no heard a whole lot about Greenock.
That's near Glasgow.

In Scotland.

Youse can google it later.

Estonia's got this border, with Russia, it's three-hunner kilometres long but – it's no exactly been *agreed.*
They're no exactly in agreement about where it is – starts, finishes, that kinda thing.

We was there to reassure our allies.
We're very reassuring, the British infantry.

In actual fact, we was a tripwire.
No one wanted anything to kick off. No NATO. No the Russians.
But if it did, we would just stop them rolling unchallenged into Estonia.
Cos the thing about the Russian army is – there's hunners of them. Really, a lot.
And bear in mind, this is after Trump pulled out.
Nice image that.

Our first tour of duty, we were fresh out of training. Fresh meat.
Wee Alison Cormack –

This gallus big lad Brian Armstrong. Hard man on the
surface, soft as a doughnut underneath.
Some wild Welsh woman with the filthiest mind on the
planet.
Our Sergeant, a London geezer, first I'd ever met. Best I'd
ever meet.
An me.
Side by side in a platoon of twenty-five men.

McLeish was top dog – he *was* a hard man. Impressive guy,
an smart, an he *never* let his guard down. Don't fuck with
him. Follow his lead, that kinda guy.
Best pals with O'Connor who was, basically, a sociopath.
Totally unpredictable. And with no fear whatsoever. Of
anything. Except cling film. Hated the old cling film, did
O'Connor.

She shifts her gaze, looking into the middle distance.

I was ten when I first met her. Ten years old.

She was on a bike wearing this ludicrous outfit of tutu an
trackies an those plastic wee jelly shoes. She's trying to do
tricks – but she's no Danny MacAskill.
She catches me watching, an for a second I realise I must a
been sneering or looking disdainful you know, cos for a wee
moment she looks hurt but then it vanishes, melts away that
look an she grins – 'You want a shot?'
I go 'I'm no dressed daft enough.' Testing her.
She's still grinning: 'Your clobber looks stupit enough tay me.'
I look down, I'm wearing head-to-toe Nike.
I go over, she haunds me the bike. And I've watched the
boys do it an I'm a quick learner so I start bouncing the
wheels around an doing beginner tricks in no time.
And I know how this can go down.
I'm already better than she is on her own gear, she'll
probably no like that but –
But she's just 'You're amazing – show me how.'

After that – we pretty much did everything together.
An I knew it was the real deal when she followed me up
a mountain.

We was thirteen.
I was –
The smartest lassie in the class, an the only black person in
a sea of white folk.
(It's no very – multicultural –
Greenock.)

So I was –
Navigating, negotiating, firefighting. Surviving – just.

And the only teacher Cormack an I had with an ounce of
sense took us up a mountain when we was thirteen.
Told us we could survive up there if we wanted, if we learnt.
Small squad of us.
We all loved it.
That woman showed us more in a day –

You get the picture.

That was it fay me.
I wanted to learn to survive a mountain. Or a desert. Or a war.
Cos up there – doesnay matter where your Da was fay, when
you're fighting your way through a gale force eight.

And wee Alison Cormack, she didnay just follow me up a
mountain, she followed me –

Sounds come through the door and/or a change in the light.

– all the way to Estonia. To the edge of Europe, where if you
turn to the east there's Russia, stretching into the far
distance, bigger than either of us could grasp.

FINDLAY *looks towards the door again.*

Scene One

2022.

A field used as a training ground in a NATO army base, rural east Estonia, near the border with Russia. Mid-morning.

FINDLAY, CORMACK, DAVIES, ARMSTRONG, ADEYEMI *and* SANDS *take part in a training movement sequence. It develops into a rehearsal for a patrol.*

FINDLAY, CORMACK, DAVIES *and* ARMSTRONG *take up patrol positions, with* ADEYEMI *and* SANDS *watching.*

ADEYEMI. Too slow, Armstrong, much too slow. You're leaving Davies exposed.

The SQUADDIES *move as a group.*

Cormack, you're off by about thirty degrees. Adjust yourself. Good.

Davies, come in a bit lower. And faster. Better.

Everyone, check your positions. Check again.

They make adjustments.

All right. Relax.

You all need to be faster. And you're still leaving your arses hanging out.

Ma'am, could we practise with you now?

SANDS *comes into the group and they rehearse with her.*

Good work. Thanks Ma'am.

SANDS. Sergeant Adeyemi, I want to take it slowly in the forested area.

We're looking for really small signifiers, it'll take time.

ADEYEMI. Of course, Ma'am.

(*To the* SQUADDIES.) Good work.

(*To* SANDS.) Thanks Ma'am.

(*To the* SQUADDIES.) Any questions so far?

ALL. No, Sarge.

ADEYEMI. Good. Take on some water. We'll get you briefed in five.

SANDS *and* ADEYEMI *exit.*

The others sit to cool down. CORMACK *pulls up her trouser leg and inspects her shin.*

FINDLAY. What's going on wi yer shiny shins mate?

CORMACK. I dunno.

Beat.

FINDLAY. Let's see.

FINDLAY *goes to* CORMACK *and has a close look.*

Looks like you've picked up a tick.

CORMACK. Shite.

CORMACK *finds some tweezers in her kit bag and hands them to* FINDLAY, *who begins work on removing the tick.*

ARMSTRONG. I think ye're supposed tay use Vaseline.

FINDLAY. What?

ARMSTRONG. Suffocates them, then youse pull them out when they're deid.

FINDLAY (*to* CORMACK). Mate, you got any lubricant?

CORMACK. No, ma friend.

FINDLAY (*to* CORMACK). Could be worse. Couple I know went hiking an got ticks in their bits.

DAVIES. Both sets of bits?

FINDLAY. His an hers.

CORMACK. Grim.

FINDLAY. Had tay extract them fay each other.

DAVIES. That's a romance-killer.

FINDLAY. Darn tootin. Tweezers out, trousers down, I'm never gonnay look at yer genitals the same way again.

ARMSTRONG. They could a done wi the Vaseline tip.

CORMACK. Imagine, ticks in yer fanny.

DAVIES. No thanks.

CORMACK. Embedded in yer fl– /

FINDLAY. *Mate!* (*Pulling it out.*) There you go.

CORMACK. Oh what a beast!

ARMSTRONG. Gee us.

FINDLAY *hands him the tick.*

Oh Christ, that's so big I can see the glint a Lyme disease in its eyes.

He's taken his sock off and is waving his foot around.

Cormack?

FINDLAY. Oh, Christ. No this again.

CORMACK *approaches his foot.*

Fucking wean.

CORMACK. Ah, leave him alone.

FINDLAY. He's treating you like his mammy.

ARMSTRONG. She's good wi feet.

(*To* CORMACK.) Do I need crutches?

You bitches could be ma crutches.

FINDLAY. Hey!

DAVIES (*looking out of the window*). Here they come.

CORMACK. Yer toes are fine. Put yer boot back on.

He puts his boot back on.

ADEYEMI *and* SANDS *enter.*

ADEYEMI. Don't let us rush you, Armstrong. Take as long as you need.

ARMSTRONG *hurries with his boot. The* SQUADDIES *sit.*

SANDS. Good. So, let's recap.

Our patrol is a night-time reconnaissance to investigate possible military activity in the border area.

I know normally one of my team would come out with you, but I need to see this for myself.

The only civilians normally here are the local farmers and their families. But there has been evidence of activity in the forest that looks like the normal pattern of life has changed.

Could be the local teenagers having parties.

Could be homeless people setting up camp.

Or it could be covert meetings.

Pro-Russian locals and Russian army.

We need to know.

Most men round here are farmers and tend to dress accordingly. What does that mean?

FINDLAY*'s hand goes up.*

SANDS. Findlay.

FINDLAY. Civilian footwear. Nay tattoos.

SANDS. Right.

DAVIES *raises her hand.*

ADEYEMI. Davies.

DAVIES. Seriously, Ma'am. I'm not being funny, but I know a whole load of farmers who have tattoos.

ARMSTRONG. She's no talking about Wales ya numpty.

SANDS. And does anyone want to tell me what they picked up from the warning order?

Beat.

FINDLAY. Leaving at twenty hundred hours an moving at four klicks per hour in darkness, we can cover ten klicks arrive at our destination at zero three hundred hours.

Moon state, one quarter waxing. So very dark.

SANDS. Good. Anything else?

FINDLAY. Forestation is medium density. Average temperature at night, eight degrees. Average precipitation twenty-five per cent.

Possibility of bears.

DAVIES (*alarmed*). *What?*

ADEYEMI. There are no bears Davies.

SANDS. Thank you, well observed.

ARMSTRONG. How she *do* that?

CORMACK (*proudly*). She's got a wee camera brain: click, click, perfect recollection.

ADEYEMI. Cormack. Talk us through the navigation points. What grid reference are we getting to?

CORMACK *can't find her notebook.*

SANDS. Where are your notes? No? Come on then Armstrong.

ADEYEMI (*to* CORMACK). See me after.

ARMSTRONG. E4.

ADEYEMI. Correct.

SANDS. Armstrong, you are the section 2LC and in command of the multiple, correct?

ARMSTRONG. Aye Ma'am.

ADEYEMI. How many klicks till we get to the edge of the forest?

ARMSTRONG. Two an a half.

ADEYEMI. Where are our report lines?

DAVIES and ARMSTRONG *flipping through their notebooks, trying to read their own writing,* FINDLAY *has hers closed.*

ARMSTRONG (*to* FINDLAY). Go on Einstein.

She ignores him.

DAVIES (*to* FINDLAY, *out of the officer's earshot*). Fuck's sake, you'll save us hours of fannying around – go on.

ADEYEMI *is watching.*

ADEYEMI. She's right – Findlay?

FINDLAY. End of the forest section – Polar, jus before we jump ower the stream – Cinnamon, an at final destination – Grizzly.

SANDS. Good. Sergeant Adeyemi?

ADEYEMI. Last rehearsals commencing in half an hour, field at the back. See you there. Thank you Captain Sands.

The SQUADDIES *attend to their kit.*

FINDLAY (*to* CORMACK). Has McLeish been hiding yer stuff again?

CORMACK *ignores her.*

DAVIES. You need to tell him to fuck off. Or you talk to him Brian, he's your mate.

ARMSTRONG. Mebbe it's time we telt someone.

FINDLAY. No.

ARMSTRONG. How?

FINDLAY. We need tay know it ends cos they learnt tay respect us, no cos they were telt.

ADEYEMI *approaches*.

ADEYEMI (*to* CORMACK). What was all that about? It's not like you to be slack with your kit.

Beat.

Anything I should know?

FINDLAY. No Sarge!

CORMACK. No, Sergeant Adeyemi. Sorry, Sergeant Adeyemi.

ADEYEMI. All right. You were asked.

ADEYEMI *exits*.

Scene Two

Same location, immediately afterwards. All rehearsing the patrol. ADEYEMI *is correcting the* SQUADDIES *when they move at the wrong speed, get details wrong, etc.* SANDS *is observing. They rehearse the transition from moving in single file to fanning out when reaching a more exposed area.* DAVIES *drops down first.* ADEYEMI *follows, touches* DAVIES' *heel and goes to the right five metres.* ARMSTRONG *follows, touches* ADEYEMI's *heel and then goes five metres to the left.* CORMACK *is last and taps* ADEYEMI *on the shoulder before she takes her place. There are various mistakes that* ADEYEMI *corrects.*

The rehearsal ends.

ADEYEMI. So as per, we're not expecting anything to happen out there.

But just to make sure everybody gets it let's go over the actions on. As practice.

Actions on illumination?

Anyone?

ARMSTRONG. Take immediate cover. In a ditch if necessary.

ADEYEMI. In a shit pit if necessary. And illuminations would include?

FINDLAY. Car headlights, house lights, enemy flare.

ADEYEMI. Actions on coming under fire?

FINDLAY. Go down intay cover, look fay the enemy, wait fay fire tay cease, make sure nay more fire incoming an then proceed.

ADEYEMI. Correct. We do not want to get involved in contact with anybody. Understood? Everyone clear?

ALL. Yes, Sarge.

ADEYEMI. Captain Sands, anything else before we move on?

SANDS. Yes. Information manipulation is a key tool for them. Be aware of any conversations, people or situations that strike you as out of the ordinary.

And just a final reminder about social-media accounts. They could hack electric toothbrushes if they wanted to. No slip-ups please.

ADEYEMI. Thank you Ma'am. Patrol dismissed.

ADEYEMI, ARMSTRONG *and* DAVIES *exit*. FINDLAY *is about to go but* SANDS *stops her.* SANDS *and* FINDLAY *alone*.

SANDS. You pay attention, don't you Private Findlay?

FINDLAY. Yes, Ma'am.

SANDS. Also – I've seen your shooting scores. They're marksmanship standard.

FINDLAY. Thank you, Ma'am.

Beat.

SANDS. Have you ever sat an IQ test?

FINDLAY (*bursts out laughing*). Sorry Ma'am.

SANDS (*smiling*). I'll take that as a no.

Would you like to?

FINDLAY (*emphatically*). No thanks! Ma'am.

SANDS. So, you haven't thought about career progression?

FINDLAY. Ma'am?

SANDS. Because the others defer to you.

I've noticed.

Beat.

Any thoughts on becoming an officer? It might suit you – Sandhurst. There's a route you could take.

FINDLAY. *Sandhurst?*

SANDS. Yes.

FINDLAY. Ooft.

SANDS. I know, it's a very formal place. But you'd be surprised.

I went there, and I wasn't sure.

But turns out, you just spend a whole year learning new things.

Beat.

FINDLAY. Why me Ma'am?

SANDS. I think you've got what it takes.

FINDLAY. Thanks Ma'am. But I reckoned I'd work ma way up.

Sergeant, then mebbe RSM one day. Mebbe.

SANDS. Sure. And nothing wrong with that.

But what I'm talking about is commissioned officer rank – gives you the future chance of a commanding officer role.

FINDLAY. I appreciate that Ma'am, thanks.

But it's no fay me.

I love – being part of a team.

SANDS. You'd still be part of a team, but you'd be leading it.

FINDLAY. Oh sure.

An thanks. But here's the hing Ma'am – folks complain aw the time about how they hate what they do.

I love what I do.

Every bit of it.

Fay day one.

Felt at haime.

So, I think I'll stay where I am.

SANDS. I understand. You've just arrived after all. Give it some time, keep it in mind. Okay?

FINDLAY. Thank you Ma'am.

FINDLAY exits as ADEYEMI *re-enters.*

ADEYEMI. Happy Ma'am?

SANDS. Yes.

Beat.

I see Cormack's struggling.

ADEYEMI. Not at all Ma'am.

SANDS. She didn't have her notebook.

ADEYEMI. Yeah, bad timing – but she's normally very organised.

Beat.

SANDS. Sergeant Adeyemi, I overheard them at the end there.

Sounded like there's an ongoing issue.

Beat.

ADEYEMI. Couple of the lads in C platoon have an attitude problem.

SANDS. But nothing's been reported?

ADEYEMI. Nope.

SANDS. They don't want to stand out.

ADEYEMI. They won't even tell me.

SANDS (*kindly*). I'm not surprised.

It's shameful, not being able to solve these things yourself.

They want to earn your respect.

ADEYEMI. Yeah.

SANDS. What do you think it consists of?

ADEYEMI. I don't really know, girls won't say.

Had some problems before in the platoon but I stamped on it hard. But it's like whac-a-mole, innit? Smash it down in one place and it sticks its ugly head up somewhere else.

Beat.

I want the girls to tell me.

SANDS. What's your best guess?

ADEYEMI. Cormack seems to be a target. Someone's hiding her stuff.

There's hand gestures the boys think I can't see.

They're playing music with – dirty lyrics when they know the girls are about to arrive in the NAAFI.

Leaving porn playing on laptops.

I don't even know what else.

And I don't know who's leading it – it'll only be a couple of them.

But it only takes a couple of them.

SANDS (*ruefully*). So the cultural change and leadership programme hasn't quite worked then?

ADEYEMI (*adopting the same tone*). Not quite.

SANDS. Can I do anything to help?

ADEYEMI. Thanks Ma'am, but you know how it is, needs to be sorted in our battalion.

SANDS. Of course.

ADEYEMI. You know what – I'm gonna speak to the Ops Officer again.

SANDS. Good – so you should.

ADEYEMI. Once we put a stop to this nonsense, they can get on and have a proper career.

Beat.

SANDS. Sergeant Adeyemi, they've clearly worked hard. But we both know, if those women stay here in infantry, at least one of them will end up leaving early, injured.

ADEYEMI. They passed all the tests, Ma'am.

SANDS. I know.

ADEYEMI. There's lads in this platoon that struggle with their fitness. Some barely scraped the entry tests. Those three? They have put every ounce of everything they've got into this. I've never seen anything like it. Resilient doesn't even cover it.

SANDS. I am not disputing that.

But think of the long term.

The reports show explicitly that the injury rate is going to be *very* high for these women, over time.

They're twenty years old.

They aren't thinking beyond Christmas let alone how their lives will pan out.

What happens to them when they can't be soldiers any more because of the pain they're in?

Can't do the sports they love. Maybe struggle with childbirth. Life-long pain.

Beat.

ADEYEMI. They've been taught how to look after themselves.

SANDS. Which will benefit them.

But you can't change how their bodies are built.

Beat.

ADEYEMI. I'm with them every day, I might not know what the other lads are saying but I know what kind of people they are, and what they're capable of.

SANDS. What they *want* to be capable of.

ADEYEMI. Ma'am, the only thing that's going to stop them reaching their potential as soldiers is starting to believe they can't do it.

Starting to believe the drip, drip, drip that they'll never be quite as good as the men.

SANDS. You really believe in them.

ADEYEMI. Yes, I believe in them.

You know what it's like to have assumptions made about you twenty-four-seven.

Gets in your head.

Then you blame yourself for having let it get in your head.

Then you have to fight hating yourself.

Then you have to build yourself up again.

It's – a lot of work.

Course they're capable of it.

But too much negativity and it's gonna stop them performing.

SANDS. I hear what you're saying.

I just think they shouldn't get their hopes up about how long this is all actually going to last for them.

I think they deserve to know the facts.

ADEYEMI. They know themselves.

SANDS. They're only twenty Sergeant Adeyemi.

ADEYEMI. They're soldiers Ma'am, they're bloody good
soldiers.

Scene Three

*The forested border of Estonia and Russia, on the
reconnaissance patrol. The same day, very late at night.*
FINDLAY *and* CORMACK *huddle at the edge of a clearing.*

FINDLAY (*on her in-ear radio*). Whisky three zero send over.
(*Listens.*) Received. Whisky three zero out. (*To*
CORMACK.) About two minutes till they're here.

Sands is staying wi the guys at the front.

Fine-looking trees.

CORMACK. Strong, good girth.

FINDLAY. Been around a while, know how tay handle
themselves.

CORMACK. Getting tay that stage aren't we?

FINDLAY. Well you shouldnay cage a tiger.

Fucking wouldnay be noticing those French lads if we had
some real purpose out here.

CORMACK. Idle haunds make for /

FINDLAY. A lot of wanking.

You know normally I go fay older men? But those French
boys.

CORMACK. Sweet baby Jesus.

FINDLAY. Great eyes. Lots of pride /

CORMACK. Tho – they're aw arrogant as.

FINDLAY. Dinnay lecture ma fanny, it's got nay sense.

Unexpected bonus this, the odd wee stroll through nature.

CORMACK *strokes a tree*.

Stop harassing the forest Cormack.

CORMACK. So what did the grand Captain want wi you?

FINDLAY. She jus fancies me.

CORMACK. Oh aye. Here, hold this.

She holds out her weapon and FINDLAY *takes it from her. She pulls her trousers down, squats to pee.*

FINDLAY (*irritated*). This'd better no be when conflict starts. I'm no having you sent haime cos you got shot in the arse.

CORMACK. I'm more worried some insect's gonna climb up ma stream.

FINDLAY. Uh-uh. They dinnay do that. Ticks are the ones tay watch out fay.

CORMACK. Ach, it wasnay that bad.

FINDLAY. Mate, you know what Lyme disease is?

CORMACK. When you drink tay much Lilt?

FINDLAY. It'll be less fucking funny when ye're hospitalised.

CORMACK *stops peeing, pulls up her trousers and stands*.

You've pished on yer kecks.

CORMACK (*looks down. Not concerned*). Oh aye.

What did Sands want?

FINDLAY. She's aw intay me being a commissioned officer – Sandhurst.

CORMACK. Fuck up!

FINDLAY. Aye.

CORMACK. That's amazin!

FINDLAY. Oh come on, we jus got here. It's bullshit.

CORMACK. No, it's no.

FINDLAY. What's the big fucking hurry anyway?

Does she think she's sent tay save me?

(*Does posh* SANDS *voice*.) Well those are excellent scores /

CORMACK (*also does posh* SANDS *voice*). For a girl –

FINDLAY (*posh* SANDS *voice*). Full marks on your shooting –

CORMACK (*posh* SANDS *voice*). You're very good –

FINDLAY (*posh* SANDS *voice*). Is it because you have been in a street gang?

CORMACK (*posh* SANDS *voice*). Crack, have you tried crack?

ARMSTRONG *and* DAVIES *enter.*

FINDLAY. Gents.

CORMACK. Ladies.

ARMSTRONG. How's it hanging?

FINDLAY. Jus enjoying the nature, you know.

ARMSTRONG (*on his in-ear radio, to* ADEYEMI). Romeo two eight send over. Received. Romeo two eight out.

Said couple more minutes then we'd be moving on.

This night-time nonsense is playing havoc wi ma vit-D levels.

I need some *sun*, man.

DAVIES. Faliraki.

FINDLAY. You know what? I dinnay gie a fuck where we go next, as long as there's nay goats.

CORMACK. Those *rancid* goats.

DAVIES. Aw, but those goats love Armstrong, don't they mate? Did you two know this? Dunno what he's been doing to those goats man, but see every time we're on patrol, soon as we get within eyeshot of them, they all pick up their weird little heads and start bleating, then they're all making maximum speed in our direction like we've got fuckin goat nip in our pockets. What do you do to them?

ARMSTRONG. Dr Dolittle isn't it? Animals jus love me.

CORMACK. That's no love mate. Ye're a goat-groper.

FINDLAY. That's exactly it. They can tell he's shag hungry an they come running ower.

DAVIES. So it's goats does it for you, eh, Armstrong? Personally, my thing is a girl who doesn't speak a word of English and looks good touching her toes. That's just my thing.

ARMSTRONG. Mine's a peachy arse. Cannay beat a peachy arse.

Beat.

Those goats have stunning arses.

FINDLAY *points at some snapped branches at shoulder height.*

FINDLAY. Hey – sign there's been someone moving through here recently –

CORMACK. We'd better note that fay yon intelligence woman.

ARMSTRONG. Oh boy, would I smash that!

CORMACK. She's about fifty man.

ARMSTRONG. Aye, so double the gratitude. Listen lasses, I've gotta let it out somehow – stuck bunking up wi youse is cramping ma – (*Gestures wanking.*) style.

It's getting bad, man. Getting critical. A critical mass. What about you girls, you havenay had any fay months have you? You must be suffering an aw.

CORMACK. No really. We can get oursels off without youse ever knowing.

FINDLAY *gestures at* CORMACK *to stop talking.*

CORMACK *doesn't notice*.

ARMSTRONG. Fucking good fay you! Mebbe we should schedule a threesome –

CORMACK (*covering her ears*). Too much man!

ARMSTRONG. Och, you say that but she's intay it. (*Nods at* FINDLAY.) She keeps coming tay me in the night.

FINDLAY *ignoring him*.

You get up an start tiptoeing around ma bed. I can hear you.

FINDLAY. That's called going for a pish Armstrong.

ARMSTRONG. Right at the end of ma bed. Aw gentle footsteps n that. If you kick the end of ma cot I'll take the hint an make ma move.

FINDLAY. That would be inadvisable.

ARMSTRONG. I can read hints fay the bints. Wee non-verbals coming through. I'm listening girls.

FINDLAY. Talking of pish, ye're kneeling in Cormack's.

ARMSTRONG *reacts and tries to move the position of his knees; the others amused*.

ARMSTRONG (*into his radio*). Romeo two eight send, over – (*Listens.*) Romeo two eight out. (*To the others.*) Right we're moving.

They move off.

FINDLAY. This is a full-on forest, eh?

I guess Scotland used tay be like this.

CORMACK. Scotland *is* like this you fud.

They arrive at the edge of a clearing. They train their night visions on what's ahead, and see a car, abandoned, in the middle of the clearing.

ARMSTRONG. Civilian vehicle.

CORMACK. Why is that there?

FINDLAY. Is anyone in it?

ARMSTRONG. I cannay see anyone.

DAVIES. Na, me neither.

ARMSTRONG. Jus abandoned then?

DAVIES. It's a brand new car. Don't leave that lying around in the forest.

CORMACK. Mebbe it's /

Sound of a baby crying.

FINDLAY. Listen!

ARMSTRONG. What is that?

DAVIES. Is it an animal?

CORMACK. Sounds like a wean.

DAVIES. Is it in the car?

ARMSTRONG (*on the radio*). Hello whisky three zero this is romeo two eight. We've found a civilian vehicle, possibly occupied. Twenty metres west of the bridge.

Over.

Listening, trying again.

The boss is out of range.

The baby crying.

CORMACK. That wean's no happy.

ARMSTRONG. Where's the Ma? What do we do?

FINDLAY. Don't do anything. Jus wait.

CORMACK. What fay?

FINDLAY. Till we get hold of Adeyemi.

DAVIES. There's smoke.

CORMACK. Oh Christ, the fuel tank –

FINDLAY. It's no gonna blow up, is it?

Clare?

DAVIES. I've no idea, not from over here.

ARMSTRONG (*trying again with the radio*). Fucking radios.

He moves a couple of steps away from the others, trying to get ADEYEMI *on the radio. The baby crying.* CORMACK *starts to move across the clearing.*

FINDLAY. Stop.

ARMSTRONG *turns and sees what* CORMACK *is doing, hesitates, tries to work out whether he should stay close to the others or try and get the radio to work.*

CORMACK. If there's a chance, even a wee one, that car's gonna blow we should go an get the wean.

FINDLAY. Disagree. It could be some kinda set-up.

CORMACK. We cannay wait tay find out.

FINDLAY. We have tay, Cormack.

CORMACK *shakes her head and continues to move across the clearing.* ARMSTRONG*'s continued dilemma.*

ARMSTRONG. Mate, we should wait.

CORMACK *pauses and turns. The baby wails again.*

CORMACK (*to* FINDLAY). How sure are you?

FINDLAY *stares at her.*

I'm going.

CORMACK *continues walking.*

FINDLAY. Alison – don't.

CORMACK *ignores her and continues across the clearing.*

DAVIES. Come back –

CORMACK *reaches inside the car and lifts something small.*

ARMSTRONG. She's got something. She's got the baby! Oh Cormack, you legend.

CORMACK *straightens up, holding the thing she's picked up. She turns towards them.*

FINDLAY. It's no real. It's – it's a doll.

It's no real!

DAVIES. A *doll*?

Suddenly there is incoming gunfire from the direction of the border.

CORMACK (*dropping down to a squatting position*). Oh fuck!

The others react instantly – ARMSTRONG *makes a decision and runs off a couple of metres to try and get a signal for the radio;* DAVIES *and* FINDLAY *drop down and aim their weapons towards the border.*

DAVIES. Who goes there!

Beat.

FINDLAY. Advance an be recognised!

ARMSTRONG *has got a signal and moves back as close as he can to the others while keeping the signal.*

ARMSTRONG. Hello aw stations, contact. East fay across the border area. Several shots. Shooter no seen or identified. Foxtrot one nine is exposed. Advise. Send. Over.

Boss is within range.

He readies his weapon.

FINDLAY. Cormack, stay still, I'm figuring this out, okay?

FINDLAY *slowly gets to a kneeling position then silently signals to* CORMACK *to move to the back of the car.*

CORMACK *starts to move. There is another round of gunfire. She gets to the back of the car, making it a barrier between her and the gunfire, and takes cover.* FINDLAY *signals that it is a rifle and the direction the shots are coming from.* ARMSTRONG *and* DAVIES *raise their weapons in the direction of the shooter.*

Dinnay return fire.

ARMSTRONG. *What?*

CORMACK. Who is it?

FINDLAY. It's a rifle. Dinnay return fire.

ARMSTRONG. Fuck is it? Do you think it's them?

FINDLAY. Almost certainly mate.

They're trying to provoke us.

If they'd wanted tay have killed her they'd have killed her.

CORMACK. The car's really hot. The metal's hot. I can feel it.

DAVIES. That's not good.

DAVIES *and* ARMSTRONG *look at* FINDLAY. *She is calculating.*

FINDLAY (*to* DAVIES). Is it gonna explode?

DAVIES. Maybe.

FINDLAY. When?

DAVIES. Could be any minute. Or not. I don't know!

CORMACK *remains in a crouching position, her gun at the ready. Horrible tension amongst the others.*

FINDLAY. Ye're alright mate. Dinnay return fire.

ARMSTRONG. She's out there in the open.

(*On the radio.*) Aye Sergeant, another round. Okay. Romeo two eight out.

(*To the others.*) He's staying up ahead. Make sure Sands is okay.

Suddenly there's another round of gunfire. Flames start to spring from under the car bonnet.

CORMACK. Oh, Christ man.

FINDLAY. Stay where you are.

ARMSTRONG (*on the radio*). Believe enemy is attempting to provoke us to return fire.

Okay. Romeo two eight out.

Says use our judgement.

CORMACK. What's going on?

FINDLAY. Stay where you are.

Wait it out.

DAVIES. Till what?

FINDLAY. Till they give up.

ARMSTRONG. They're gonna kill her.

FINDLAY. Nope.

They want us tay fire.

It's what they want.

ARMSTRONG. I'm no sitting here while she gets shot in the face.

FINDLAY. She's no going tay get shot in the face.

They wait.

CORMACK (*quietly*). Ma leg's wet.

DAVIES. Smell the liquid.

CORMACK *slowly moves, puts her hand down and touches the liquid, brings it back up to her nose.*

CORMACK. It's petrol.

FINDLAY. Okay, we'll bring her back.

ARMSTRONG. Agreed.

Another burst of gunfire. It takes out one of the car headlights and at the same time ignites the petrol. There is a small explosion sound and a proper fire starts in the car.

CORMACK. Do something!

FINDLAY. Okay mate, come back, low as you can, fast as you can. Go!

CORMACK *starts moving back. More gunfire comes from the border, and a bullet hits a tree very close to* CORMACK.

He's inconsistent.

She takes her time, aims carefully, then shoots. The incoming fire stops.

Scene Four

The squaddies' mess. The following day, early morning.

ARMSTRONG, DAVIES, CORMACK *and* FINDLAY *are sitting, waiting.*

FINDLAY. Dinnay start, Davies.

DAVIES. A *fake* baby Cormack.

CORMACK. I cannay believe I fell fay it.

DAVIES. You and me both!

FINDLAY. Shutit Davies. No one knew what was going on.

ARMSTRONG. Can we give it a rest?

DAVIES. First tour and you disobey orders on because of a baby. That's not even a fucking baby!

CORMACK. I thought it was real!

FINDLAY (*to* CORMACK). You did good mate. (*To* DAVIES.) An you need tay shut it.

ARMSTRONG. Look lassies, we aw get tay say our piece in a wee minute. So till then… can we jus… thank you.

Beat.

DAVIES. So what we gonna do then?

Beat.

CORMACK. What do you mean?

DAVIES. Are you ready for the fallout? Walked in the NAAFI there and O'Connor and that bunch were all – (*Cradles a pretend baby and does waa-waa noises.*)

CORMACK. I'll jus ignore it.

DAVIES. Oh really, will you? Great. But it's not just about you, pet lamb. They did it to *me*.

All of us been tarred with your daft brush.

FINDLAY. We need tay show a united front.

DAVIES. United about what a prick Cormack is?

FINDLAY. Hey –

DAVIES. Was it just me out there telling her *not* to run into no man's land?

CORMACK. If you didnay like what I did then we can talk about it.

DAVIES. Oh, I *really* don't like what you did.

To the others, this time turning away from CORMACK.

Maybe you're happy with the notion of sitting in the transport, riding towards who-knows-what with full hatred coming off the lads. Maybe you think it won't affect you. It fucking will. Huge distraction. You'll make mistakes I *promise*. It's *dangerous*.

Beat.

FINDLAY. We say we think she's a legend an did the right thing.

We say we're proud of the risk she took.

That they can bitch an moan when they've had their first contact.

DAVIES. Proud?

FINDLAY. We need tay stick together an ride this out heids held high.

DAVIES (*to* ARMSTRONG). She's right.

We don't have a choice.

We can't slag her off. They'll think we're typical two-faced bitches.

Fucked either way eh?

Beat.

FINDLAY. Brian?

ARMSTRONG. Aye alright, jus thinking ma way through this.

Beat.

So listen, I'm down wi the she's-a-hero angle – on one condition.

FINDLAY. Oh aye?

ARMSTRONG (*nodding at* FINDLAY). That youse stop hauling me ower the coals fay every wee comment an titty joke I come out wi.

Beat.

FINDLAY. Why the conditions mate?

ARMSTRONG. Why?

Beat.

See the shit I havetay take off them, fay bunking up wi youse? Hanging out wi the lassies?

FINDLAY. So?

ARMSTRONG. I fight yer corner every day.

DAVIES. So what, you want a *reward*?

ARMSTRONG. You think I wanna be called *Briony* aw the fucking time?

Asked why I've no even fingered one of youse yet?

Asked if I've started ma period yet?

Eh?

DAVIES. Well, now you know what it's like. So dry your eyes.

ARMSTRONG. Oi! You want O'Connor in here? Or McLeish? Cos you carry on wi that nonsense an I'll be out of here an you'll be bunking up wi one of those animals. That what youse want? You think they'll let you sleep in peace?

A long silence. CORMACK *is distracted, searching for something.*

CORMACK. Where the fuck are they?

Ma headphones?

He's taken them. He's been in here.

He's been in ma personal stuff an he's fucking taken them.

I cannay get tay sleep wi out ma tunes an he fucking knows it. I telt him.

ARMSTRONG. You telt McLeish that?

CORMACK. Aye that's why he's gone an taken them, so I'll no sleep.

ARMSTRONG. Right, that's enough. He's gone too far, coming in here.

Let's you an me go down there an sort this.

I'm gonna kick fuck outta him.

CORMACK. Brian, he'll kill you.

If he doesnay O'Connor definitely will.

ARMSTRONG. No if we aw go. Come on Davies.

They turn to look at her. She is holding up some headphones.

DAVIES. Are these yours? The red ones?

The others stare at her.

Sorry, there was a City match on.

Others still staring at her.

Were you really going to go down there like the Dirty Dozen?

Amazing.

I wish you could all see yourselves, about to strut out the door.

Beat.

ARMSTRONG. Aye me an ma three dirty bitches off tay save the world.

FINDLAY. Is that one of those filthy comments we're never allowing you?

ARMSTRONG. Aye, aye it is.

FINDLAY. Wee bit tame to be honest mate.

ARMSTRONG. Alright.

So ma first wank was tay the notion of Lorraine Kelly.

Fucking Lorraine Kelly.

FINDLAY. There's something wrong wi you.

CORMACK. First person made me come was a happy-hardcore DJ called Kevin.

FINDLAY. Oh Christ /

DAVIES. Helen Mirren.

CORMACK. Who?

ARMSTRONG. What?

FINDLAY. You fancy the *Queen*?

DAVIES. She's smoking. Even at seventy.

You look at her photos and you can practically *smell* her cunt.

I like those women-of-the-world types. When you first meet them they're all, 'What can you show me, eh?'

And then they leave the scene of the crime all grateful and damp panties – know what I mean?

ARMSTRONG. So we both intay older women then aye?

DAVIES. I'm just basically into fanny, Armstrong, not that bothered if it's young, tight and fresh out of school or saggy and sophisticated. It's all fanny.

ARMSTRONG. Nay cock ever?

DAVIES. Never seen the point, really. Sorry mate.

ARMSTRONG. That's okay, you lot make great porno, so I'm no bothered.

CORMACK. Brian, they're no actually /

ARMSTRONG. Lesbos?? Jesus mate, give me some credit.

They look towards the door; FINDLAY *tense,* ARMSTRONG *fidgeting,* DAVIES *pacing.*

If any of youse are interested, Sands is ma type.

CORMACK. No interested.

ARMSTRONG. When she's up there being aw stern. Fucking hell.

FINDLAY. Officer.

ARMSTRONG. So?

FINDLAY. Off-limits.

ARMSTRONG. Really aye? Cos I was gonna ask her come tay Nando's wi me Saturday.

FINDLAY. No literally you prick. Davies, come on –

DAVIES. I'm not gonna police his wank bank darling.

FINDLAY. Ach, come on, you must be sick as I am of having females get up an be all ballin an the first hing the lads say when they've exited the room is I would or I wouldnay.

ARMSTRONG. That's how we do it man!

FINDLAY. What?

ARMSTRONG. Cos it pure winds you up.

FINDLAY. No it's no, it's /

ARMSTRONG. Ach, alright you've got me, it's cos it stops us thinking like our mammies are telling us off. Female like her up there, makes us feel like wee people again, aw vulnerable – dinnay be cross Mammy. But say they're a ride an then they're no yer mammy any more.

FINDLAY. Fucking weans the lot of youse.

ARMSTRONG. Aye weans with big dangly dicks.

DAVIES (*to* ARMSTRONG, *low sexy voice*). I met your Ma.

Beat.

When we passed out.

ARMSTRONG (*serious*). Back off Davies.

FINDLAY *and* CORMACK (*whooping*). Do it, do it Davies!

DAVIES. She's got a lovely… haircut.

Beat.

There's something very – Helen Mirren about her. Must be that she's regal.

She gestures with her hands – half royal wave, half weighing a pair of tits.

Like the Queen.

ARMSTRONG. She's a Catholic you cunt.

CORMACK. She was really kind tay me that day. Could see I was pure nervous on parade an she gave me a sweetie. Telt me I looked really smart an tay jus imagine the Major naked an I'd be fine.

DAVIES. You see /

ARMSTRONG. Aye she's a lovely lady ma Ma.

DAVIES. I'd /

ARMSTRONG. I'm warning you /

FINDLAY. We've found his boundaries, thought he had *none*.

ARMSTRONG. Hey, I'm yer Lance Jack, remember?

CORMACK. Play that card while you can Brian, she'll be yer boss this time next year.

DAVIES. What's that now?

CORMACK. Oh aye. Guess what Sands said tay her?

FINDLAY. Wheesht.

CORMACK. Don't be embarrassed /

FINDLAY. I'm no /

CORMACK. They want her tay go tay Sandhurst.

Beat.

ARMSTRONG. Fuck up!

Talent-spotted eh.

Good fay you, wee genius heid.

Beat.

DAVIES. Well, that's something isn't it.

FINDLAY. I said naw.

CORMACK. Idiot.

FINDLAY. I'm no interested.

CORMACK. Yeah but /

FINDLAY. Shut up man – seriously. They dinnay wanna hear about it. *I* dinnay wanna hear about it.

ARMSTRONG. Let's talk about someone else's Ma.

Beat.

FINDLAY. Mine's a really quiet wee woman. No says much in company. But see if you get her pished, get a couple of rums in her an she brags about this time she had a smear test /

CORMACK. You might need tay explain that particular procedure tay /

ARMSTRONG. What did I jus say?

I know what a cunting smear test is.

CORMACK. Sorry. Ma bad.

FINDLAY. An she was telt by the nurse she had a lovely cervix.

Beat.

DAVIES. What does that even mean?

FINDLAY. Aye it's no yer everyday compliment.

DAVIES. And she tells folk that at parties?

FINDLAY. Yup.

CORMACK. Bet she does it tay wind yer dad up.

FINDLAY. You think? That's underhand man.

Christ, youse lot might be a nightmare but at least I'm away fay that bunch.

DAVIES. That why you joined, Findlay? Get shot of the family?

FINDLAY. No, man.

Round ma way, team I hung out wi, the boys would drive tay the top of the car park – there's this bit where the perimeter wall's gubbed an there's nay barrier: third storey. They'd drive tay the edge full speed an the first tay shout stop was a poof. Christ – the front wheels hanging off the edge sometimes. I wanted tay get involved. They said 'Oh aye Sarah, no bother, if you sit on Gerro's knee, he'll hold you nice an tight.' Well I thought tay mysel, that sounds like a full breach of health an safety regulations.

Beat.

Fucking drive the car now lads. An get paid tay do it.

CORMACK. She borrowed ma Ma's car an raced those boys tay the extreme edge of the car park.

DAVIES *high-fives* FINDLAY.

What about you, Brian?

ARMSTRONG. My Da's forces. It's a good living. Plus he was drowning in pussy fore he got married.

Same for you, aye, Davies? Pussy?

DAVIES. No mate.

Was desperate to get away from the tractor chat and valley commandos. Pontardawe was a class place to grow up, don't get me wrong: I can fix any one of the John Deere 5R series with one hand tied behind my back. I just didn't want to spend the *whole* of my life in a dank field in the middle of nowhere surrounded by retards.

So that plan worked well, didn't it?

Beat.

You proud of your dad then?

ARMSTRONG. Course.

DAVIES. Ho, Findlay, you aspire to be like your Ma?

FINDLAY. Oh definitely.

I always wanted tay grow up knackered an bitter.

DAVIES. Me too, daydreaming of being divorced, skint –

FINDLAY. Nay time tay see ma mates.

DAVIES. Only place I'd have any fun would be at work –

FINDLAY. In a basement –

DAVIES. Minimum wage –

FINDLAY. Threat of getting the sack any second –

DAVIES. Threat of a tit-squeeze from the boss if he caught you alone in the corridor –

FINDLAY (*fake shock*). Does that still go on!

ARMSTRONG. Aye I'm forever feart one of you sex-starved lassies is gonna grab ma boabie in the shower block.

FINDLAY. In yer dreams Brian, like any one of us would go within a mile of the diseased cocks of any of the scummy lads in this platoon.

Beat.

Sorry Ally.

CORMACK. Dinnay be sorry. It was in basic, I didnay know which company he'd be in. I didnay know he'd be in the same platoon as me. An I definitely didnay know he'd turn out tay be a pure bully.

DAVIES. Jesus.

CORMACK. Holding it ower ma heid aw the time. The threat of aye cunt knowing.

ARMSTRONG. Seriously, mebbe now's when Adeyemi should be telt what's going on.

DAVIES. Armstrong. If Sarge digs about he'll find out she shagged McLeish then all our reputations are fucked.

No one can ever know Cormack, you're just gonna have to suck it up.

What was the point, eh? What was the point of 4 a.m. marches till you were sick on yourself, burpees for breakfast, for a year? Having fish put in your pack for a month? The whole lot of them – (*Mimes jiggling breasts.*) while we're completing an assault course? Hhhhmm?

They're waiting aren't they? Half the platoon, half the officers, thousands of old-timers and twice as many internet trolls – they are all waiting for us to fuck up so they can say, 'Told you so.'

Silence from the others.

Scene Five

ADEYEMI*'s office, immediately afterwards.*

All present.

SANDS. Let's start from the beginning.

> *The four* SQUADDIES *move into the same positions as at the start of Scene Two; and move in exactly the same ways as they did in Scene Two – hand movements, head turns, all the same as they speak their lines.*

CORMACK. We was moving forward, observing our surroundings as we moved.

SANDS. And there was nothing out of the ordinary at this point?

DAVIES. Trees were thinning out, so we stopped to check what was ahead.

ARMSTRONG. Saw an abandoned car through the night visions. It worried me.

CORMACK. Thought it was a weird place tay leave a car.

FINDLAY. Couldnay see a driver, or passengers – was wondering if folk were hiding in it, behind it.

DAVIES. It looked abandoned, so wondering if there'd been a collision.

ARMSTRONG. Hearing this noise. Baby noise.

FINDLAY. We couldnay tell what it was.

DAVIES. I thought it might be an animal.

CORMACK. Armstrong heard a baby crying, Ma'am. There was a baby.

SANDS. A baby?

DAVIES. A car with a noise coming from it. I knew there was something wrong with it.

FINDLAY. Spooky situation alert. I'm reckoning it's a possible threat, but mebbe no.

CORMACK. It sounded exactly like a wee baby. In distress.
I was thinking about why it was crying, what we should do.

ARMSTRONG. The radio wasnay working.

FINDLAY. Reckoning eighty twenty it's a come-on. Trying tay
work out what the most likely explanation was. An I telt the
others – take no action.

SANDS. And you went to investigate?

CORMACK. We could see smoke coming fay the bonnet.

So aye, I did.

FINDLAY. Smoke coming fay a car can mean a dozen hings.

DAVIES. She shoulda waited.

Beat.

ARMSTRONG. Findlay's telling us aw we should wait till we
got hold of Sergeant Adeyemi Ma'am.

An it was pure torture, trying tay get a hold of him – thinking,
how many steps would I have tay go tay get the signal?

DAVIES. I couldn't tell at that distance if the smoke indicated
a potential explosion. It was so dark.

FINDLAY. Cormack moved across the clearing tay the car.

CORMACK. Sarah called me back /

ARMSTRONG. Putting herself in harm's way.

DAVIES. Findlay said out loud what I was thinking – this could
be a trap of some sort. And not to walk into it.

ARMSTRONG. I was thinking – mebbe she's right – Cormack
– tay do something, but then I looked ower at Findlay – she's
never been wrong.

Wean's wailing again, clogging ma thoughts –

Evidently, go an get the wean.

DAVIES. It was obviously a trap, Ma'am.

FINDLAY. I'm telling her no – she's exposed in the clearing.

She's no listening.

Jus walking out intay the open.

I feel sick.

DAVIES. We hadn't made a collective decision.

ARMSTRONG. I couldnay get a signal.

Fuck!

CORMACK. I was at the car, Ma'am, middle of the clearing. I could hear the baby crying, I looked inside the car an there was jus this doll.

ARMSTRONG. She held it up Ma'am.

I'm grinning.

You legend, you've saved it.

CORMACK. It wasnay a baby.

DAVIES. It obviously wasn't a baby.

FINDLAY. There was no baby.

ARMSTRONG. It was like one of those dolls aw ma sisters had, that make a real sound – you know, tay put you off getting pregnant.

They dinnay work.

DAVIES. That's when the shots came, Ma'am.

FINDLAY. Adrenalin shot pumping through me.

Aw I wanted tay do was fire back.

Trigger finger trembling.

But I didnay.

ARMSTRONG. Hard as fuck, moving away fay the lassies, but three paces an I get it – secured the signal.

CORMACK. I scrambled tay the back of the car, try tay get something between me an the incoming.

SANDS. How many rounds?

CORMACK. No sure, Ma'am. Loads.

DAVIES. Two rounds.

ARMSTRONG. Seemed like a couple.

FINDLAY. Three rounds. It was a light weapon Ma'am. Rifle.

I telt the others no tay return fire.

SANDS *looks up sharply.*

She's out in the open.

I'm ninety per cent that's a skilled marksman.

But he's no shot her.

Coulda – but hasnay.

What's he want?

Only hing makes sense is he wants us tay fire back.

Playing wi us.

Provoking us.

So we mustnay.

Beat.

Unless there's something I'm missing.

I cannay get this wrong.

I can see her shaking wi fear.

I cannay get this wrong.

ARMSTRONG. Hear his voice coming back at me, the relief. Update him.

He's staying wi you Ma'am.

Tells me we need tay decide fay oursels.

CORMACK. They're shouting tay each other, about who it might be, the shooter /

DAVIES. It was chaos.

FINDLAY. Asking Davies what kinda danger the car was.

CORMACK. Armstrong was yelling about who was shooting –
an I wis saying I needed tay get out of there.

FINDLAY. I telt her tay stay still.

CORMACK. I'm really exposed, jus – in the middle of this
wide-open space.

DAVIES. Then there was another round.

She said the car was hot.

CORMACK. But this time it was worse – hit the groun near me
– felt like they were saying – next time it'll be you we hit.

FINDLAY. Then there was another round of incoming fire,
seemed it was even closer tay Cormack.

DAVIES. Must have ignited something. Cos then there were
flames coming from the car.

ARMSTRONG. I was thinking – they're trying tay kill her. Jus
waiting, it was horrific.

FINDLAY. I knew what was at stake Ma'am.

DAVIES. Findlay's saying not to fire back.

Her best friend out there.

That's –

I respect her for doing that.

CORMACK. Another round.

ARMSTRONG. She was shouting, sounded desperate. Jus
leaving her there –

FINDLAY. There was a lull.

That was the worst.

Stay calm, stay focused.

But I'm breathing like I've jus finished a marathon.

Heart's going nuts.

DAVIES. We were just waiting.

ARMSTRONG. Then she said her leg was wet.

More gunfire.

DAVIES. She was calling out.

FINDLAY. Ma gut tells me dinnay fire back.

I *know* they want that. I *know* we mustnay.

They're no gonna kill her, I know they're no.

An if I'm wrong?

CORMACK. Do something!

ARMSTRONG. She was trying tay get back.

CORMACK. I could feel the bullets cut the air /

FINDLAY. I realised he's mebbe gonna hit her without meaning tay.

He wasnay trying tay kill her – but he might anyhow.

I hadnay thought of that.

That he mebbe had a job but might no be very good at it.

I hadnay thought of that.

I'd got that wrong.

I aimed an fired.

Beat.

CORMACK. It stopped.

ARMSTRONG. Nay more rounds.

DAVIES. Reckless, she was.

Beat. SANDS *surveys them.*

SANDS. Okay – dismissed.

ADEYEMI and the SQUADDIES all slowly leave the room, FINDLAY is last. When the others have all gone she turns back.

SANDS and FINDLAY alone.

FINDLAY. Permission tay ask a question Ma'am.

SANDS. Go ahead.

FINDLAY. What will the enemy do next? Will they use it fay PR Ma'am?

SANDS. They may, yes.

Beat.

You did the right thing out there.

FINDLAY. Okay. Thanks Ma'am.

Beat.

SANDS. How have rest of the platoon reacted?

FINDLAY shrugs.

I take it not well.

Beat.

FINDLAY. It's cool.

I jus need tay handle it the now an once the tour's properly kicked in they'll chill out, nay doubt.

SANDS. You shouldn't have to put up with this. You were promised fair treatment. Weren't you?

I'm guessing that's one of the reasons you're here. You were told you'd be judged on merit. That once you were selected, once you'd been trained, all that respect would be given as default.

FINDLAY. I jus want tay get on wi ma job Ma'am.

SANDS. Of course you do.

Beat.

Private, you should know – it may not change.

Yes, your platoon will probably settle down and get used to you.

But when you become Corporal, Sergeant – move up?

Or your lot join a different battle group?

That's a new bunch of people – and the same problems over again.

FINDLAY (*joking*). I'm hoping by then ma reputation will precede me Ma'am.

SANDS. Sure. Quite right.

Beat.

Whatever you're putting up with right now – it doesn't happen in the Intelligence Corps. In my Corps.

FINDLAY. Yeah?

SANDS. Yes.

FINDLAY. Why is that Ma'am?

SANDS. Because for us talent is rare, important and we know it when we see it.

Someone like you would be truly welcomed.

FINDLAY. Ma'am?

SANDS. I would *never* normally do this.

It's poaching and Major Ahrens would rightly be furious.

But I can see you being wasted here and I hate it.

You have *enormous* potential Private Findlay.

You'd do really well in Intelligence Corps.

Beat.

FINDLAY. Do you think I dinnay belong here Ma'am?

SANDS. No, that's not what I mean.

I don't think *they're* ready for someone like you.

ADEYEMI *arrives with a look of urgency.*

ADEYEMI. Ma'am –

SANDS *takes one look at the expression on his face and exits hurriedly with him.*

FINDLAY (*to audience*). She was right tay be worried.

A farmer'd been shot deid, on the other side of the border territory.

That's what they said.

A *farmer*?

Really?

Shooting at us, several rounds, deliberately, in the dark?

That's no an auld fella feart fay his livestock.

That's military.

So – ma first kill.

Or no.

Cos even though there was footage of his body an his wife wailing an his weans bubbling, Sands telt me that it was possible it wasnay true. A hoax.

But – we didnay know.

So, mebbe I'd killed someone, mebbe I hadnay.

Farmers dinnay shoot at soldiers wi accuracy in total darkness.

No where I'm fay anyway.

But –

I'll never know.

Mebbe that poor wee woman wi a headscarf, howling tay heaven an her scared-looking weans bawling their eyes out, mebbe I was the cause of that.

An I'll *never* know.

By the afternoon that footage was everywhere.

Every channel, every feed, in every continent.

An along the border, aw hell broke loose.

•

Scene Six

ADEYEMI*'s office, the same day, late at night.*

All present.

SANDS *addresses the whole platoon/audience.*

SANDS. They've mobilised.

Their allies have given them confidence.

President Xi Jinping made a statement this morning saying the Russian Federation has the right to protect its borders and its people.

Most likely COA is that they mobilise to the east of the border, their side, as a show of force. Probably along the whole length of the border, ground and air cover. It is assessed that they won't cross the border.

As Major Ahrens told you we depart at zero three hundred hours.

A male, aged approximately twenty-five years, from the Estonian Russian community was killed last night in Povka. He was beaten and stabbed. We believe it was more than one perpetrator, with links to the local militia.

So civilians are scared and the atmosphere is volatile.

Most dangerous COA is that militia forces supportive of Russia will clash with the Estonian Defence League.

We may see street battles, properties being vandalised and robbed, more civilian casualties.

We want to avoid that.

We expect additional air and land support by zero eleven hundred hours.

Beat.

Now I'm going to hand you over to Ops briefs.

ADEYEMI. The rural population within ten klicks of the border will be evacuated.

That will commence at zero four hundred hours.

The civic groups we've been training will lead that, with support from A and C platoons.

Our job is to go to Predka – the first town outside the evacuation area. To try and reassure the civilian population; stop the militias causing more trouble.

Any questions so far?

Indicating a map fixed on the wall.

We'll enter the town from the west and patrol west-east, down Katarina Street, as far as the Orthodox Church. Distances of twenty metres apart, stay away from side streets and stay in contact. We'll cover five hundred metres till we get to the main square, then regroup on the west side of the town hall. Then hold for ten minutes. We'll continue patrol east-west, down Katarina Street covering the same ground again.

To provide reassurance.

Understand?

ALL. Sarge.

Beat.

ADEYEMI. The RF vehicles and heavy weapons will be at the border by zero six hundred hours tomorrow.

Okay?

ALL. Yes, Sarge.

ADEYEMI. Right, that's it.

Get some rest.

I need you at your best.

ALL. Sarge.

ADEYEMI *and* SANDS *exit.* CORMACK *has her head in her hands.*

DAVIES. What's done is done. Come on mate. We're all in this together. Okay?

FINDLAY. Come on Ally.

CORMACK (*irritated.*) Mate!

ARMSTRONG (*quietly, to* FINDLAY *and* DAVIES). Give her a minute.

DAVIES *and* FINDLAY *gesture their agreement and exit together.*

CORMACK. I'm sorry Brian.

ARMSTRONG. How?

CORMACK. It's cos of me aw this is happening.

ARMSTRONG. What, that we're getting some action finally?

I'm fucking delighted.

CORMACK. Ha-di-ha.

You know what I mean.

Us four getting aw this nonsense. At least one person's deid.

I made a giant error man – the others are right.

I mean, I'm no sorry for what I did an if I'd been a guy nay one would a given a shit that it was a dolly in that car but –

I was still hasty.

I feel like a fanny.

He goes to her, pushes her shoulders down.

ARMSTRONG. Hey! What's aw this heavy glum stuff?

Pretends to push weight off her shoulders.

Let's get rid of it.

No need.

It was always gonna be complicated youse lot being here.

No yer fault.

I think you were really brave, going out tay that car.

She nods and smiles up at him. Beat. He goes to kiss her. She leaps away from him.

CORMACK. What the fuck!

ARMSTRONG. Sorry.

ARMSTRONG *shocked at the vehemence of her reaction.*

CORMACK. Seriously, what the fuck?

ARMSTRONG. I'm sorry, okay?

He takes a couple of paces away from her.

So that never happened, right?

CORMACK. Dinnay try an turn it intay a joke Brian.

It's no okay.

ARMSTRONG. I'm ower here, I'll stay ower here.

CORMACK. Aye, do that. Jesus.

Beat.

ARMSTRONG. So am I no good enough fay you?

CORMACK. *What?*

ARMSTRONG. You heard me.

CORMACK. That's – do you think fay a second I'd do anything wi anyone in ma squad?

Do you really?

D'ya think that of me?

ARMSTRONG. I didnay /

CORMACK. *Fuckin* hell Brian.

ARMSTRONG. Why you so *angry*?

CORMACK. You know what happened before, imagine if the other lads –

ARMSTRONG. How would they know?

Do you think I'd *tell* them? Those animals?

Beat.

I dinnay think you understand how bad it could get.

It's fair tay say you got unlucky. That McLeish an O'Connor hate the idea of youse lot.

That's bad luck.

But I'm houding them back.

What ye're getting is level-one nonsense. It could be so much worse.

CORMACK. Houding them back?

ARMSTRONG. If I was wasnay pals wi the two of them there'd be nothing stopping you being destroyed by those lads. It'd be relentless.

But I'm reminding them daily ye're ma buddies an they're tay houd back.

So no – I'd no be telling them if anything happened between us.

CORMACK. Brian – I –

ARMSTRONG. Why McLeish Ally?

The way he talks about females.

Why him?

CORMACK. That's no how he spoke tay me.

Beat.

He's scared. Of – being close tay folk. Of being gentle.

ARMSTRONG. He's practically wearing a T-shirt saying 'I'll fuck you then spit on you' an lassies are always going fay it. No wonder he thinks nothing of burds.

CORMACK. He reckons he has to behave that way.

ARMSTRONG. Oh man, I had no idea.

I thought – I thought you jus – I didnay realise you actually cared about him.

CORMACK. I don't *care* about him. No now.

ARMSTRONG. Okay.

He's really no a good guy.

CORMACK. Brian, I know!

The shite he's put me through since we got here.

ARMSTRONG. Exactly! He'll fuck you an then /

CORMACK. Stop saying that!

Beat. ARMSTRONG *goes to her again, stand close and looks down at her. She gently shakes her head.*

ARMSTRONG. So you jus dinnay fancy me. That it?

Beat.

CORMACK. No enough. No enough tay risk –

ARMSTRONG. But you'd risk it fay McLeish.

You know what's utter shite? If it werenay fay me telling him he cannay he'd have telt aye cunt in Estonia what you looked like in the skud. An way worse.

I think I was expecting you tay say youse was so drunk you couldnay see an you regret every second of it.

But you dinnay, I can tell.

I think you'd do it again if you thought you could get away wi it.

Beat.

Feels like the kinder I am, the less love I get.

I didnay know it worked like that.

Scene Seven

Outside the squaddies' mess. The following day, not long after midnight.

ARMSTRONG, FINDLAY, CORMACK *and* DAVIES *packing the last of their kit and loading their weapons in preparation to leave.*

FINDLAY. Cormack – how many socks you taking?

CORMACK. Two.

FINDLAY. I'm taking three. I'm no having wet feet again.

ARMSTRONG (*catches a bit of skin while he's loading a bullet*). What the absolute fuck!

No one's interested in his pain. Turns his attention to his rations.

I've got meatballs /

FINDLAY. Aye I've heard that about you.

ARMSTRONG (*trying to retain his dignity*). Macaroni an pasta.

DAVIES. Macaroni *is* pasta darlin.

(*To* CORMACK.) You done yet?

Everyone looks at CORMACK. *She's not paying attention.*

Cormack?

Come on, now /

FINDLAY (*offering help*). Do you want /

CORMACK. Jus checking ma ammo, Jesus!

Beat.

FINDLAY. Tomorrow's making us aw tense man – dinnay take it out on me.

CORMACK. Tomorrow's no making me tense. Dinnay put words in ma mouth Findlay.

FINDLAY *is visibly irritated.*

ADEYEMI *and* SANDS *enter.*

ADEYEMI. All right? Nearly done there?

FINDLAY. Aw good.

ADEYEMI. No more than two pairs of socks.

SANDS. How are we?

ADEYEMI. Never better, Ma'am.

SANDS. It's normal to have a few nerves, remember.

ADEYEMI. Na – this lot are animals.

They're excited not scared.

You haven't seen their wild side yet Ma'am.

SANDS. I'm sure.

ADEYEMI. Take Cormack here.

CORMACK. Sergeant Adeyemi please –

ADEYEMI (*to the squaddies*). What's a good illustration of Cormack's wild side, lads?

Beat.

DAVIES. When she stayed up half the night to dig a booby trap behind the shit pit in the Brecons cos some of the lads were calling her double-D?

ADEYEMI. Yes – that!

FINDLAY. Ma favourite's the titty-bar story.

DAVIES. Oh yes!

CORMACK. I'd rather we didnay /

FINDLAY. Like a kind of urban legend. Saved McLeish fay having his limbs pulled off by a bouncer.

ADEYEMI. Oh, no I don't know this one. Please share.

CORMACK. No – no in front of – Captain Sands, Sarge.

SANDS. Oh absolutely in front of Captain Sands.

Findlay?

FINDLAY. Oh I wasnay there – this is one for big Brian.

Long beat. ARMSTRONG *glances at* CORMACK, *who is looking down.*

ARMSTRONG. Ach, I'm no so sure you wanna tay hear this one.

DAVIES. Don't be a tool, mate.

It's a belter, Ma'am.

ARMSTRONG. You really want me tay tell a night-out story tay Captain Sands?

ADEYEMI. Yup.

During ARMSTRONG*'s story they continue to finish loading their weapons and packing their bags.*

ARMSTRONG. So it was a Thursday. Me an Cormack are out for a quiet pint an we get a call. Go an join them. There's three of them there, Jonno; that one looks like he's got a nutritional problem, dinnay know his name – an Private McLeish.

They'd been there days by the look of it.

ADEYEMI. *Days?*

DAVIES. Y'know what McLeish's like sir.

ADEYEMI. What *is* he like?

DAVIES. He's one of the most entertaining, abstract-minded cunts I know.

Sorry –

SANDS. Not a problem. I've known some abstract-minded cunts in my time.

The SQUADDIES *shocked and amused.*

DAVIES. So your excellent value Private McLeish after eight hours on the piss –

ARMSTRONG. Aye, so we hi up tay that titty bar near the station – Cormack's idea, actually – get tay the door an the bouncers all 'boys – you been drinking?'

Hing is, Jonno an the skinny fella – they're practically foaming at the mouth, something out of the living deid.

An I'm peering at the bouncer an I'm thinking c'mon, *look at them*, drink is the least of their problems.

An then Cormack spews out this little speech, eloquent as fuck, bout how they wouldn't enter an establishment known for its quality, truly high-class minge –

He stops, glances at SANDS *and she nods that he can continue.*

– in the condition of a bunch of alchies, cos they are as respectful of the Muffle Club – that's what the place is called – as they are of the esteemed profession of the doorman. An the bouncer almost buys it when Jonno starts swaying like a daft tree. I'm busy trying tay right him when Cormack jus switches intay sober.

An goes, 'Listen mate; we've had a couple, as you'd expect, but these are decent lads an no going tay cause any trouble, we jus want tay come in an enjoy ourseles.' Giant pause then the big guys aw, 'Okay – in youse go.' An we're practically at the coat check when Jonno jus stops where he is an projectiles an actual fountain of vomit.

Course the bouncer is ower in a shot an Cormack is in there again. 'This man has defended his country on three continents. If he wants tay spew on yer cheap-arse carpet, he has more than earned the right.'

Which is total shite, we're still in training, but they dinnay know that an fore long we're getting a free veterans-only lap dance; which is no actually that great as the burds there are minging but hey, we're no paying.

An Cormack's at the bar telling war stories.

ADEYEMI. Now that's teamwork.

Beat.

DAVIES (*to* ADEYEMI). Sergeant Adeyemi – it's not really fair on us if you get to hear how we fell over and made idiots of ourselves and we don't hear your tales of woe.

ARMSTRONG. Aye right enough, surely you've fallen off a tank or something –

DAVIES. Slept in for parade –

SANDS. Maybe Sergeant Adeyemi's record is unblemished.

ADEYEMI. Blemish-free.

DAVIES. It's gotta to be blemished. I mean, you're a legend not a *saint*.

Beat.

ADEYEMI. I was locked in a toilet once. Really locked – had to break out through an air vent.

ARMSTRONG. *What?*

ADEYEMI. In Mombasa. After a night on the shots.

ARMSTRONG. Vodka?

ADEYEMI. Sambuca. And tequila.

DAVIES. That's suicide!

ADEYEMI. I was seeing in triplicate. Every idiot in the bar, but times three.

I must have fallen asleep on the toilet cos I woke up and the lights are off and the bathroom door is locked on the outside. It was this big hotel bar and they'd just shut the thing down for the night.

Obviously I tried the standard reverse breaking-and-entering. But nope. So I'm scanning the room and the only thing I can see is an air-con vent in the ceiling and I'm not spending the night on my own in the lavvy so luckily the vent's above one of the cubicles. So I stand on the toilet, pull off the cover, climb up.

I elbows and kneed it down that shaft for about ten minutes thinking this is not the glamorous life I planned for myself when suddenly the thing collapsed.

DAVIES. Christ!

ADEYEMI. Fell right into the hotel kitchen – on to their prep table. Bunch of local chefs wielding meat cleavers staring down at me. They all started screaming their heads off and waving their weapons. Then my hangover kicked in. I thought I was going to have a haemorrhage so I rolled off the table, spotted the nearest exit and legged it.

ARMSTRONG. Those heady rookie days, man.

Beat.

ADEYEMI. It was last year.

Laughter.

SANDS. The PrideInn?

ADEYEMI. Yeah!

FINDLAY. You been tay Kenya? Ma'am.

SANDS. Yes but it was actually just R and R from a Somalia posting.

DAVIES. Somalia!

ARMSTRONG. It's radge there eh?

FINDLAY. How many times you been Ma'am?

SANDS. Six times.

DAVIES. Whoa, that's a ton.

ADEYEMI. Excuse me, Ma'am, I'm due with Lieutenant Dawson.

ADEYEMI *exits*.

SANDS. I've specialised in the region.

DAVIES. Interrogating Al Shabaab?

SANDS. Yes.

DAVIES. Oh.

FINDLAY. So you know some of the local languages Ma'am?

SANDS. *Si sax ah*.

FINDLAY. Is that Arabic?

SANDS. Benaadir.

ARMSTRONG. Ooft.

FINDLAY. But you speak Arabic too?

SANDS. *ana afeal*.

FINDLAY. How many languages you speak?

SANDS. Five.

ARMSTRONG. Five! Jesus! I can barely speak one!

CORMACK. Who's Al Shabaab?

FINDLAY. Like Al Qaeda, but Somalia style.

CORMACK. Hardcore Islamists?

FINDLAY. Aye.

ARMSTRONG. Do they no have a hing about no talking tay females?

SANDS. Correct.

ARMSTRONG (*without thinking*). So how were you allowed tay interview them?

SANDS. Allowed?

ARMSTRONG. Sorry, Ma'am, really sorry I /

SANDS. It's okay. There's often an assumption that it's pointless putting a female officer in a room with an Islamist militant.

That they won't speak to us.

FINDLAY. But they do?

SANDS. Well yes, sometimes.

At first it's hard to make the case that you should do those kind of interviews. Until a certain point. There's usually a particular moment in your career that mean things change.

FINDLAY. Ma'am?

SANDS. Oh, it's not very interesting, I'll tell you another time, we can grab a coffee.

FINDLAY *smiles and looks down, pleased but embarrassed.*

DAVIES. I wanna know!

Beat.

SANDS. Okay.

I was on a base a few kilometres from Mogadishu, providing support to the commander about what the threat picture looked like. There was a regular patrol of a derelict that overlooked the base, and one day, someone was there, a local man – claimed he was the janitor.

But they couldn't prove it so they brought him in.

The nearest other Ints Corps officer who had interrogation training was fifty hours away. General flurry, what are we going to do now?

I suggested I speak to him – I've got the right training. There was reluctance, then they said I could give it a go – but there was no way I was going in there on my own. So it was me and the infantry Captain. He led the way. I took a pen and paper. The janitor ignored me, I took some notes. But their conversation wasn't really proceeding. I waited until they'd said all they really could to each other.

Then I asked him about local feeling, local networks – what I'd been researching and thinking about there for months.

I was able to speak to him in his dialect. His defences were down with me – he didn't think I was in a position to cause him harm or decide what would happen to him. Then he begun to realise the opposite – that I could help him. Help him prove that he wasn't a real threat, help him get out of that room. I'd been there long enough to have figured out what someone like him might be motivated by.

And he begun to understand that it was possible to exchange information with me for something he needed. By that point he couldn't care less if I was a woman. I was his possible avenue out and that's all he was thinking about.

He wasn't a janitor, of course.

And he turned out to be very useful to us.

After that I was asked to interview men quite regularly.

DAVIES. Boom.

Somalia, eh Ma'am?

Wild.

Captain Sands and I were talking armoured vehicles earlier. Apparently the armoured corps out there have got some insane bits of kit. Who knows, maybe I'll fuck off to that lot, get away from you losers.

FINDLAY *looks sharply at* DAVIES. SANDS *becomes aware she may have made a mistake.*

SANDS. So – how are we feeling about tomorrow?

No one speaks. ADEYEMI *enters.*

It may be your first proper contact, but you will excel.

Do you know how many people can do what you do?

Beat.

Most twenty-two-year-olds are wanking to a manky poster of Taylor Swift and working out how they'll be able to afford new trainers.

You can march for seven hours then defend your country.

You're going to be fine.

ADEYEMI. Ma'am – battlegroup HQ need to talk to you.

SANDS *nods at the* SQUADDIES *and exits.*

Patrol is delayed, we're not going out for a couple of hours.

Beat.

Let's use it to get in the right head space.

ADEYEMI *exits.* CORMACK *exits before she has a chance to be alone with the others.*

ARMSTRONG. I'm gonna take an enormous shite.

DAVIES (*as he's leaving*). From your enormous hairy arsehole.

ARMSTRONG. Yep.

ARMSTRONG *exits.*

DAVIES. Those two have fallen out, haven't they?

FINDLAY. Something's up, aye.

DAVIES. We can't fall apart mate. Not right now.

FINDLAY. I'm well aware.

DAVIES. And I've never seen Cormack backchat you like that, what's going on?

Beat.

You know, sometimes I've wished you two *would* fall out.

FINDLAY. What?

DAVIES. It's not easy being the third prick at the lady party, you know?

FINDLAY. Ah.

Sorry mate, if we've ever made you /

DAVIES (*gently*). Shut up.

But you've got to sort it love.

You two have to stay tight.

We could implode if you don't.

So go and cuddle her or whatever weird we've-known-each-other-from-before-we-grew-tits stuff you do, and sort it out, okay?

Scene Eight

Flat roof of the accommodation block, immediately afterwards.

CORMACK *is doing parkour. After a few beats* FINDLAY *appears, climbing up the ladder.* CORMACK *sees her and stops briefly, then carries on.*

FINDLAY. When we get back fay fucking around out here we're heading tay the Highlands, you an me.

CORMACK. What?

FINDLAY. Can pitch a tent anywhere you like an then that's yer territory. We'd a fucked that up a couple years ago, we'd of ended up water-logged, an freezing, an squaring up tay stags on moors an that, but now – it's our birthright mate. Let's take the Hoolie 2 an go feral.

CORMACK. Alright but I'm in charge of rations.

FINDLAY. How?

CORMACK. Seriously?

FINDLAY. I can fucking make sandwiches mate.

CORMACK. Aye, aye they're delicious but ye're so good at navigating an kit maintenance it's a waste of yer skills tay be on cooking duty. Mate.

FINDLAY. Fine, you can be wifey.

CORMACK. Are we sharing a tent but?

FINDLAY. Cos ma snoring?

Ah, you wish you could snore like me.

Beat.

What's going on wi you an Brian?

You fallen out?

CORMACK. Wee bit.

FINDLAY. We canna /

CORMACK. Ach, stop fretting.

People fall out.

Beat.

FINDLAY. Did she speak tay you an aw?

CORMACK. Who?

FINDLAY. Sands.

CORMACK. What about?

FINDLAY. Other regiments.

CORMACK. Oh aye – she chatted tay me about being a medic. Talking about courage under fire, that kinda thing. How?

FINDLAY. She's fucking poison.

CORMACK. What?

FINDLAY. She tried tay get me tay go ower tay Intelligence.

She telt me she would never normally do that – never try an poach someone, our secret et cetera. Then she was aw – come tay Intelligence Corps, they don't love youse here.

Beat.

CORMACK. So?

FINDLAY. Christ, did you no clock she's been chatting up Davies an aw? Telling her about aw the fun she'd have in armoured corps?

She's on a mission man – she's wanting us *aw* out of infantry.

She doesnay think we can do it.

CORMACK. Why do you care what she thinks?

FINDLAY. Tell me what happened wi Brian, I should know.

CORMACK. How?

FINDLAY. Cos we're going intay a dangerous situation. We need tay be solid. The four of us.

CORMACK. Oh aye. An show the rest of the lads we're aw better than them, I get it.

FINDLAY. No mate.

Jus no prove them right.

They're *expecting* us tay be emotional, sloppy, scared – fall out wi the one man on our wee team.

Beat.

CORMACK. I remember when you didnay give a fuck.

You was more fun then.

FINDLAY. What happened wi Brian Alison?

CORMACK. He tried tay *kiss* me.

FINDLAY. Are you kidding me?

CORMACK. I know man.

FINDLAY. Naw – it's bang out of order, but did you no see it coming?

CORMACK. What?

FINDLAY. I mean, he shouldnay have, but – come *on*.

CORMACK. Whadda you mean?

FINDLAY. Way you are wi him.

You play nursey fay him, listen tay his wee problems, giggle at his jokes.

Way you act wi a lot of the guys.

Sorry mate, but it's true.

Aw cute wi them.

You get them haime safe fay Seventh Heaven fuck's sake /

CORMACK. Hold on.

I'm jus being mysel.

FINDLAY. Well yoursel is a problem then.

CORMACK. Oh come on /

FINDLAY. You cannay be doing shit tay please them out here /

CORMACK. What the fuck?

Ye're all in their faces twenty-four-seven saying 'Let us be, an respect us no matter what.'

An when I'm jus mysel you tell me I'm fifty shades of wrong!

FINDLAY. Okay.

Plain English.

CORMACK. Don't patronise me /

FINDLAY. But ye're no getting it!

I'm ower here showing them we're marching an killing machines and you're ower there being aw princess unicorn.

CORMACK. Jesus /

FINDLAY. We cannay just be oursels out here! Guard completely down, like it's the two of us at haime.

Don't be daft.

CORMACK *shakes her head in disagreement.*

Problem is mate, we need tay kinda agree on this cos what you do affects me an aw.

CORMACK. You know what? Mebbe your big brain can be two folk at once but no mine. I wouldnay know where tay start.

An I wouldnay wanna.

If you start doing stuff based on how some other bunch are judging you, then ye're fucked.

Beat.

FINDLAY. I wish I'd never brought you along.

CORMACK. *Brought* me?

FINDLAY. Aw you had tay do was follow a simple set a rules an we'd be free tay be jus soldiers. Nay females, nay schemie girls, jus excellent soldiers.

CORMACK. Oh I'm sorry, how does that work?

FINDLAY. Once there's nay doubt we're quality soldiers, they aw have tay shut it. Imagine walking down a corridor an no wondering what folk are whispering after you've walked past, no wondering what gestures they're doing – knowing it's aw jus nods an aye, she's good, I'd want her on ma team.

CORMACK. Oh please.

I love you mate, but ye're deluded if you think that's ever gonna happen.

Blokes like McLeish an O'Connor are never gonna change their minds. Even if we were Rambo mixed wi Lawrence of fucking Arabia they'd be talking shite about us.

FINDLAY. Once they see what we're capable of /

CORMACK. They already have! We've trained wi them for ower a year mate.

I dunno what ye're asking of me.

Am what I am.

I'm no ashamed a mysel an I don't see why I should be going changing.

An nor should you.

FINDLAY. I'm already *changed* mate.

I've been changing mysel left an right since I was able tay think.

Of *course* you can alter folks' opinions of you.

Of *course* you fucking can.

You *have* tay if you're me.

Since I was able to *talk* I saw what was needed.

Watch folks' eyes when you enter the room. Who's annoyed, who's curious, who's uncomfortable.

Then you correct yoursel, no too loud, no too quiet; no too confident, but no too nice.

No too *anything*.

Wee shifts here, wee adjustments there so you get asked back, included. If ye're really lucky – respected.

An as for acting on instinct.

Fucked if I know what ma instincts are any more.

Seeing yoursel through other folks' eyes all the time.

Kinda royally screws yer instincts.

Beat.

CORMACK. Why you never telt me this?

FINDLAY. Ah Christ, *really*?

CORMACK. I dunno what tay say.

FINDLAY. Say you'll take more care of how you act.

CORMACK. Sarah, it won't. Make. Any. Difference.

Why you fretting about those idiots?

Ye're clever.

You can change aw that stuff.

Get up amongst the real big boys an do something about it.

Sands offered you the golden ticket an you were aw 'Naw,
I wanna stay down here in the ditches.'

FINDLAY. I was *born* tay do this.

CORMACK. Were you fuck.

FINDLAY. I've never been happier.

Jus getting on, kit – weapons – assess what's needed – pay
attention – get on wi folk.

Uniform, boots, gun, get out there. Work out like fuck. Sleep
deeply.

Repeat.

I love it.

First time in ma puff I've felt so – peaceful.

Have you no even noticed?

CORMACK. That's no you but. Ye're gonna get bored, so soon.

FINDLAY. How the fuck would you know?

CORMACK. Cos I've been following you around since I was ten.

No cos I'm a daft sap but cos ye're so smart.

You always know what tay do.

An you tell folk.

Ye're no a stand-in-line person.

Ye're commissioned officer material whether you like it or no.

FINDLAY. Officer?

You know what that is?

That's walking intay a room that's ninety per cent men, half of which ha been tay lads-only schools an the other half voted UKIP last election.

You know what they see when I walk intay the room?

(*Exaggerated whisper.*) She's black!

CORMACK. You dinnay know what they're thinking.

FINDLAY. Do you know what would've happened tay ma reputation if *I'd* have slept wi McLeish?

Do you know what folk would've thought if I'd even have pulled ma kecks down an pished in the woods like you did?

Those are the rules I cannay break let alone the rule that says no females in charge here an *definitely* no some freaky black girl fay Greenock.

CORMACK. If you don't like it, change it mate.

FINDLAY. Oh I have been trying. Since we fucking arrived an aw you've done is make it worse.

So don't you fucking *dare*.

I should *never* have brought you.

CORMACK. You know what yer problem is?

You wan tay be part of something that doesnay want you.

You wanna be like them.

You slag them but you wanna be like them so much yer heid's upside down /

FINDLAY. Naw it's you they don't want – it's fucking low-aspiration, nay-discipline, nay-clue soft-as-fuck females like you.

CORMACK. How far would you go tay show those lads ye're one of them?

Who the fuck *are* you any more?

FINDLAY. Don't you talk shit tay me.

No when ye're washing their fucking knees an sucking their dicks for them.

CORMACK *loses control, strides up to* FINDLAY *and shoves her.* FINDLAY *steps away, tries to keep calm but can't, turns back and throws an accurate punch at* CORMACK. CORMACK *drops down for a minute but gets up quickly. They're well matched;* CORMACK *is stronger but* FINDLAY*'s anger drives her on, they fight till they are both hurt and exhausted.*

Scene Nine

An area outside the accommodation block, the same day, early morning. The sound of an engine throbbing.

CORMACK *and* FINDLAY *sitting on their packs.*

ARMSTRONG *and* DAVIES *enter.* DAVIES *sees the bruises on their faces first.*

DAVIES. What happened!

ARMSTRONG *sees their faces.*

ARMSTRONG. I'll kill /

FINDLAY. Nay one.

Beat.

We was fighting, it was us.

ARMSTRONG. *Why?*

DAVIES. Are you fit for combat?

CORMACK. We're fine Clare.

> ADEYEMI *enters, looks round at the* SQUADDIES *then approaches* CORMACK *and* FINDLAY *and looks closely at their faces.*

ADEYEMI. Show me your hands.

> *They do. He sees the signs they've been fighting each other. They drop their hands to their sides. Long beat.*

So I spend every second of my day telling the world you're a bunch of top-notch soldiers and you do *this*?

(Shouting.) Do you want me to look a fool?

FINDLAY *and* CORMACK. No Sergeant Adeyemi.

ADEYEMI. I'm really disappointed.

How stupid are you?

> FINDLAY *and* CORMACK *can't look at him. He looks at* DAVIES *and* ARMSTRONG.

And where were you two when they were playing at being heavyweights? Huh?

Can you not look after your team?

You're supposed to protect each other, you fucking *children*!

I should report this. Get one of you transferred to A platoon.

Long beat.

But I'm not going to.

FINDLAY. We dinnay want special treatment.

ADEYEMI. Don't tempt me Findlay.

(Slightly gentler.) This one time, we'll write it off as the result of undue pressure.

Got it?

You fucking wallies.

Beat.

Just be the best you can today.

And I don't mean heroics –

I need you in the game, not injured –

You hear me?

Just focus. That's all you have to do, manage your thoughts, let the training kick in – and focus.

Beat.

(*To* CORMACK *and* FINDLAY.) What you gonna say to them, when they ask what – (*Points at the bruises on their faces.*) this is?

FINDLAY. We were fighting ower which one of the lads was ugliest.

ADEYEMI. That'll do.

Come on.

He exits.

ARMSTRONG. Dinnay want special treatment? Special needs, the pair of youse.

FINDLAY. Don't you special needs me, ye're the one needs a full-time carer.

DAVIES. He bloody well will when he's done bunking with you two, you lunatics.

She goes to inspect their faces. Turns from FINDLAY *to* CORMACK.

Landed a beauty there, didn't you?

FINDLAY. I let her.

DAVIES. Have we found someone who's better at something than you are?

FINDLAY. No possible.

They all pick up their packs, begin to walk towards the exit.

ARMSTRONG. Ha! She held back.

FINDLAY. No she didnay.

ARMSTRONG. Aye she *did*.

They exit together.

Scene Ten

Outskirts of Predka, a small town near the border, sometime later.

Sound of a firefight. A few beats before ARMSTRONG *and* DAVIES *enter.* ARMSTRONG *has his arm around* DAVIES *neck, she is taking almost all his weight – he is injured, and has a lot of blood on him. They stop and catch their breath,* DAVIES *still supporting* ARMSTRONG.

ARMSTRONG. She saved ma life, she saved ma life.

DAVIES. I know, I know.

DAVIES *knows something that* ARMSTRONG *doesn't, she isn't telling him and it's a struggle for her.*

Okay get off me now.

They carefully disentangle and DAVIES *checks to see if* ARMSTRONG *can stand unaided.*

ARMSTRONG. Ye're really hench man.

DAVIES. Pull-ups paid off, eh?

DAVIES *kneels down and rolls up his trouser leg, looking at his wound. She glances up at him to let him know it's not too bad. Then she stands and runs her hand around the back of his head, looks at her hand and again looks at him to reassure him.*

You're sound boy.

ARMSTRONG (*very seriously*). Thank you.

DAVIES *can't hold his eye and he is beginning to realise she is holding something back.* FINDLAY *enters, out of breath and shaking with adrenalin. She looks at* DAVIES *and* ARMSTRONG, *registers the blood.* ARMSTRONG *sees the blood on* DAVIES' *hand. Looks at* FINDLAY.

That's no mine.

Beat.

FINDLAY. Where is she?

No one speaks. FINDLAY *squats, trying to recover her breath. They all three tensely, wordlessly wait.*

A few beats before ADEYEMI *enters.* FINDLAY *leaps up and looks at him. He stands very still and looks directly at her. She wails and crumples to the ground.*

Scene Eleven

FINLAY *alone on stage in a pool of light.*

FINDLAY. Going back over this bit is –
    But you have to, don't you?
    Otherwise it'll just swirl around in yer dream world till you lose yer shit.
    So, I make an effort to remember it from time to time, talk about it.
    So it cannay ambush me.

We were in the wee town, close tay the border.
There was anger everywhere.

No especially directed at us, though we werenay welcome.
Suddenly there were armed men on the streets, pushing past
folk just trying to get tay work, scared parents wi kids, local
football casuals wanting a taste of the action – and some
NATO troops thrown in the mix.

It was – tense.
They was just prowling the streets at first, wi occasional
bursts an clusters of fighting.
And at the beginning it was jus fists; but of course, a lot of
them had weapons.
Platoon got caught up on the main street.
We were spread out.
It was mayhem, pretty much.
Dense crowds shouting slogans an occasionally smashing
something up.
I was one end of the street – she was way far down the
other end.
So I never saw any of it.

Apparently McLeish an Armstrong get caught up between
the two sides.
In the eye of the storm of the crowd.
And it was no looking good, folk shouting abuse in their
faces.
Cormack clocked it an went in.
Opened her hands out an says 'Please, please, we all have
homes, let's go home.'
In Estonian.
She'd learnt some Estonian!
They said fay a minute or so it seemed like it had mebbe
worked, things calming down.
Most of those guys were locals, no imported militia, they
didnay want blood on their hands.
Then a rock came belting through the air, hit McLeish – an
just like that his weapon's up,
his blood's up –
An they all see that.
Then – gunshots.
Armstrong took a bullet to the leg. Goes down.

An the crowd scatter, an Armstrong's out there, alone in a
circle of space.
He'd hit his heid when he fell, he's out the count.
And Cormack's right there in a second, covering his body wi
hers –
McLeish –
I dunno, caught up in the crowd I think.

She took a bullet.
Carotid artery.
By the time anyone realised what was happening –
She'd lost most of the blood in her body.

Medic gets there, McLeish an the medic are with her –
Davies comes flying in, grabs Armstrong an gets him the
fuck out of there.

They don't know where the gunshot came fay.
Angry local?
I don't think so.
It was accurate.
And a dead female soldier makes a hell of a headline.
But I dinnay know.

I jus know she ran across the open groun tay protect
Armstrong knowing there was a shooter.
Ran out, no hesitation.
And if she hadnay, it'd probably have been Brian that bled
out in that street.
That's all I know.

Scene Twelve

ADEYEMI*'s office, a few hours afterwards.*

FINDLAY *is sitting staring at printouts of news and social-media coverage of* CORMACK*'s death.* SANDS *enters, dressed ready to leave and carrying her bergen. She sees what* FINDLAY *is doing. She puts her bag down and sits opposite her.*

SANDS. I'm so sorry.

FINDLAY. She saved his life, an *this* is what they're saying?

SANDS. Try not to read them.

FINDLAY. Look at the comments!

SANDS. Try not to.

    Beat.

    I've got some advice on security, particularly in relation to your social-media accounts.

    We can talk it through but I thought you'd probably rather digest it in your own time.

    FINDLAY *nods.* SANDS *pulls out a document from her bag and slides it across the table.* FINDLAY *reads it, expressionless. She looks up again.*

    She showed enormous moral courage out there.

    Beat.

FINDLAY. Why you trying tay get us aw out a infantry?

SANDS. I just didn't want you to feel that you had to stay somewhere that wouldn't be beneficial to you, long term.

FINDLAY. I'm no getting yer actual meaning. Ma'am.

SANDS. Statistically, you have a higher chance of sustaining more injuries than the men you joined up with.

    You know the kinds of injuries.

    Spine, joints – pelvis. Particularly pelvis.

If you sustained those injuries that'd be the end of your infantry career.

FINDLAY. Davies jus hauled Armstrong on her back ten streets. Not even a wee muscle tear after.

SANDS. Yes, but it's cumulative. This is your first tour.

FINDLAY. We're no aw gonna fall apart Ma'am.

SANDS. Statistically /

FINDLAY. Mebbe aye, mebbe no. We're in the gym every day.

No one *actually* knows anything Ma'am. About how our poor wee bodies are gonna hold up.

SANDS *stands and picks up her bergen.*

SANDS. This is a man's backpack. Designed for a man. Dimensions, strap-length, strap-location – all for your average man.

Dammit, we get given men's pants in our kit!

She throws the bag on the ground.

What does that say?

Beat.

For God's sake Findlay I am just trying to tell you what no one else will.

That they've promised you glory and equality and they *won't* deliver on it. They *can't.*

If they really gave a shit about women's experience in the army they'd talk to the women who are already serving.

You can't thrive here. And mostly, they don't care.

As long as they've trained you just enough so you can't sue them when your body finally breaks.

FINDLAY. If that's what you think, how you no speaking tay the high-heid yins, the bosses /

SANDS. I don't have that kind of power!

Beat.

I have already caused enough commotion in my career fighting for posts that would normally be reserved for men.

I am not the right person to be saying things they don't want to hear.

You can only demand things change every so often in this kind of environment.

At some point someone senior says – if you don't like it you can go somewhere else.

FINDLAY. Alison didnay lose her life so I could jus skedaddle after ma first tour.

SANDS. But you can't win.

Maybe you'll be physically okay.

But I think it's a stupid waste of your talents to fight this particular battle.

And you know what – let's say you stay, and you do well? That'll just lure other girls in, and ones who can't handle it. Who don't yet know it's a trap.

She nods at the paperwork she has given FINDLAY.

I'm leaving right now. This is the end of my time here.

My number is in there. If you want to come and work with me.

SANDS *picks up her bergen and exits.*

Sound of helicopter taking off and leaving.

ADEYEMI *enters.*

FINDLAY *looks at him for a long time.*

Scene Thirteen

2032.

Spotlight up on FINDLAY *dressed still in combat uniform but with different rank insignia.*

FINDLAY. I'd let a poison bleed intay us, but I couldnay see it at the time.
I truly do not know if I could've repaired it, the damage we'd done.
If she'd –

CORMACK, *dressed still in her combat uniform, watches* FINDLAY *from a distance.*

I looked back, and looked back, an sometimes I would think it was that moment – when I first walked past McLeish giving her a revolting look, and did nothing, said nothing. Or when Davies was hollering at her an I never stepped in. I would think it was one of those moments that started our battle /

She glances at CORMACK. CORMACK *tips her head to one side, indicates she is listening.*

But of course it wasnay one moment.
It started well before Estonia.
Started in Greenock. In the pubs, the sandstone, the docks, the men coming back fay adventures to their pissed-off wives. Started with my Da arriving decades ago, cold to the bone but hopeful. No knowing there were fights ahead of him he could *never* win. It started a long, long time ago.

We were both right.
We were both wrong.

She glances at CORMACK, *then back at the audience.*

I felt like every move we made fay the moment we joined up was important. Had an impact beyond just our wee lives. So I was studying us carefully, keeping watch on what we did. And I was right.

And she felt like what mattered was that she did right by the folk around her, an that's *all* that really mattered. And she was right.

Maybe we were both there to catch each other's mistakes. So when she wasnay there –

Ah, Christ Jesus.

I went to Sandhurst.
But no so I could join Captain Sands an her posse.
For a smart woman that was a dumb move – telling me
I couldnay do it.
Telling me it would all go to shite was like putting a motor under me.
There was no turning back then.

Went to train to be an infantry officer.
And as it happens I never got injured, ma full career.
Ma pelvis held!

Sandhurst was –
For someone like me –

An Davies an Armstrong tried to be there fay me.
They *were* there fay me.

(*To* CORMACK, *smiling*.) Weren't they?

CORMACK *smiles back*.

But the longer I was training to be an officer, the less I could be with them.

They help you to speak differently there, did you know that?
Speak proper.
And then when you get officer class, you cannay hang around with yer buddies any more.
Nope, no if they're no officers.
Just – cannay.
And I get it – it's hierarchy, it's how it works.

Back home, we'd see each other, but by then –

So I had to let them go.

I'm a Major now.
I have my own company.
Ninety-eight per cent men.
But there's a couple of females there.

And sometimes, when I'm addressing ma troops I catch the eyes of one of those females.

She looks directly at CORMACK.

And a look passes between us.
That contains so much.
Knowledge, an frustration, an fury sometimes, but also –
Triumph.
Cos, for all that – we're both there.
Me an that woman I'm looking at.
Both there.
Against the odds.

Turns back to face the audience.

I like beating the odds.

End.

A Nick Hern Book

Close Quarters first published in Great Britain in 2018 as a paperback original by Nick Hern Books Limited, The Glasshouse, 49a Goldhawk Road, London W12 8QP, in association with Sheffield Theatres and Out of Joint

Close Quarters copyright © 2018 Kate Bowen

Cover photograph by Helen Murray

Designed and typeset by Nick Hern Books, London
Printed in Great Britain by Mimeo Ltd, Huntingdon, Cambridgeshire PE29 6XX

A CIP catalogue record for this book is available from the British Library

ISBN   978 1 84842 801 0

www.nickhernbooks.co.uk

 facebook.com/nickhernbooks

 twitter.com/nickhernbooks